American Gridmark

James M. Mannon, Ph.D.

A	m	e	r	i	c	a	n
G	r	i	d	m	a	r	k

Why You've Always Suspected That Measuring Up Doesn't Count

Harbinger House
Tucson • New York

HARBINGER HOUSE, INC.
Tucson, Arizona

Copyright © 1990 by James M. Mannon
All rights reserved

Manufactured in the United States of America
♾ This book was printed on acid-free, archival-quality paper
Typeset in 10.5/14 CG 9400 Caledonia

Library of Congress Cataloging-in-Publication Data

Mannon, James M., 1942–
American gridmark : why you've always suspected that measuring up doesn't count / by James M. Mannon
p. cm.
Includes bibliographical references.
ISBN 0-943173-55-8 : $9.95
1. Achievement motivation — Social aspects — United States — History — 20th century. 2. Performance — Social aspects — United States — History — 20th century. 3. Conformity — History — 20th century. 4. Social values — History — 20th century. 5. United States — Civilization — 1970– — Psychological aspects. 6. National characteristics, American. I. Title.
BF503.M36 1989
302.5'4-dc20   89-39598
                                                              CIP

Contents

	Preface	vii
	Acknowledgments	xi
Introduction	Performance Ethic in American Culture	1
Chapter 1	Measuring Up: The Early Years	7
Chapter 2	Why Teens Try Harder: Adolescent Life in America	48
Chapter 3	The Measured Self in the Middle Years	89
Chapter 4	Losers-Weepers: Dilemmas of the Underclass	123
Chapter 5	Toward a New Vision: The Emergence of the Productive Self	149
	Notes	179

Preface

Many Americans are unwitting victims of what I call "measurement mania," an obsessive concern with measuring human life and selfhood by imposed standards of judgment and worth. What counts most now in people's lives is not so much what they can do, build or accomplish, but whether they have measured up to standards of glamor and looks, gender stereotypes, and a host of other performance evaluations inherent in an overly-organized competitive society. Americans are driven by the "performance culture," especially by an ethic that pushes people to measure their lives and worth according to the most faddish definitions of personal success, acceptability and popularity.

The result is that we are less free to find and honor genuine lives. We are less inclined to listen to the inner urgings of self or to carry out personal plans for individual accomplishment. Increasingly, we seek approval and belonging, and we crave the rewards that accompany conformity to popular measures of

Preface

success. Though we think we are free, we are controlled by the hidden and unconscious social forces of conformity.

While some Americans cope and find a comfortable existence in the "measured self," many men and women experience real doubts and anxieties about whether they can ever measure up to all that is expected of them. The adolescent female worries whether she is thin enough to be attractive to males; the middle-aged and middle-level manager yearns for one more promotion; the young mother strives to be the "complete woman," an appealing wife, quality mother and successful real estate broker. All share the anxieties associated with living up to standards and expectations that are difficult to accomplish, not of their own making and often not of their own choosing.

American Gridmark then is about life in American society in general and the downside of the performance culture in particular. Its aim is to examine how the performance ethic affects the lives of toddlers and their parents, teenagers and men and women in their middle years. My argument is that at no point in our maturation are we really free and encouraged to develop a genuinely individual existence. Rather we are constantly measured, tested, probed and evaluated to see if we have the makings for success.

This book was stimulated not only by my musings as a professional sociologist but also by my concerns as a father and husband. As a father, I am disturbed, as I think many fathers are, by my teenage daughters' preoccupation with their looks, figures and fashions. Their essential goodness and humanity lies much deeper, and cannot be measured by superficial and faddish standards. But, as a sociologist, I realize that they are gripped by "peer paralysis," and like countless other adolescents my children have difficulty finding a selfhood independent of their peer performance culture.

As one who is sensitive to women's concerns, I felt also that I

Preface

needed to address the enormous and incessant pressures on women in America to measure up to contradictory and often impossible standards of femininity, domestic expertise and career success. Women today (at least middle-class women) have great opportunities, which is laudable. But performance pressures are so severe that today's driven "complete woman" may well be tomorrow's alcoholic and anorexic. It is my contention that "having it all" and measuring up successfully in all things is an ethic quite unhealthy to those women and men, at all ages, who live for a cultural imperative rather than an inner commitment.

In a similar and more personal vein, I know my own life has been a series of evaluations in which I am being judged by standards of masculinity, attractiveness, career success and material reward. And as a college professor I have lived with pressures of the all-too-important processes of evaluation for tenure and promotion. I wanted to write a book in which other men of my age and time could identify themselves as "measured men," not very free to be what we would like or to pursue a life more on our own terms.

I'm writing for a vast number of Americans who are, I feel, tired and disillusioned with the performance ethic and all that it has done to their lives. I'm writing for those who want more than a measured self, who refuse to live up to the dictates of gender stereotypes, advertising imagery, peer culture and materialism. This book is for those Americans who would like to explore with me some alternatives.

Acknowledgments

Few books are written without abundant support and encouragement. This project is no exception and I would like to acknowledge some of the people who showed faith in me. Several faculty colleagues at DePauw were especially helpful: Nancy Davis, Deborah Bhattacharyya, David Field, Bill Cavanaugh, Stan Warren and Ruth Sargent. My university provided generous summer stipends that made possible the research and preparation of the manuscript. Eileen Johnson performed the typing duties with much skill and dedication, and provided a good deal of moral support when I needed it the most.

I've benefited as well from the love and wise counsel of my family. My daughters Sarah and Susie always had a kind word for their father and gave me keen insights into the rigors of adolescent life. My mother Lucille has given me full and loving support throughout my life. To her goes my deepest appreciation. I would also like to thank my in-laws, Freydis and Harold Stewart for their counsel, especially Freydis for her help in English usage.

Acknowledgments

My wife Sue Rice, who is everything to me, has shown me more warmth, love and friendship than I have any right to claim. I want this book to be a tribute to this remarkable woman, to whom I owe so much.

During the writing of this book I lost both my father and younger brother, Mark. I would like to acknowledge their profound influence on whatever success I've enjoyed. From these gentle men I learned much about what joy there can be in life. John White, my agent, believed in this book and helped as much as anyone in getting it published.

Some of the rudimentary ideas for this book took shape several years ago in a series of conversations I shared with my dear friend and fellow sociologist, Chuck Flynn. We had even hoped to collaborate someday on a book, as an expression of mutual concerns and long friendship. Tragically, Chuck died suddenly in 1986, far too young, talented and full of promise for such an early departure from life. With Chuck's death American scholarship lost a wonderfully creative and innovative mind. It is my hope that those who knew Chuck will see something of him in the chapters that follow, for I have tried to write a book faithful to some of the concerns we originally had in mind.

Though she deserves the dedication of this book, I know my wife will understand my desire to present it to the memory of Chuck Flynn. In many ways, he has been my guiding spirit.

American
Gridmark

Introduction

Performance Ethic in American Culture

This book is about the performance ethic in American culture, how it operates today in the lives of adults, adolescents and children, and how it results in a particularly modern personality I call the "measured self." The performance ethic is manifested early in our lives, subjecting us all to constant measurements, evaluations and appraisals, and continues virtually to our grave where our sense of ultimate worth is measured by the expense and expanse of our funeral. Because of this relentless quest to measure up to standards of health, wealth and competence, Americans are becoming less autonomous, less authentic, less real and less free.

The performance ethic is at the heart of new conformity demands in which men and women are pressured to measure their lives by external standards. At the risk of oversimplification, much of life today can be viewed as similar, but by no means identical, to life in the 1950s, an era that saw the term "peer pressure" coined. The conformity of the 1950s, the pressures to act, think and dress like everyone else led sociologist David

Introduction

Reisman to designate the "other-directed" mode as a new personality type in American culture.[1] The most vocal and respected critics of that era were the psychologists, sociologists and mental health experts who warned of the dangers in overconformity, such as the decline of national leadership and scientific and technological creativity.

The 1960s and 1970s ushered in an era, thought by many to be lasting, but apparently only temporary, with a new style of individual permissiveness in many areas of human activity. Led and inspired by the psychologists of growth, the religion of situational ethics and emerging countercultural values, people in the 1960s and 1970s were urged to break out of the bonds of conformity. What awaited them was the company of other daring Americans experimenting with new creative and innovative lifestyles centered around "growth," actualization, finding one's self, various forms of therapy and new forms of personal relatedness — living together, free love, "tuning in and dropping out." The new freedom in individual actions was undergirded by the motto, "Don't lay your trip on me." The Age of Aquarius meant that people had had enough of the "other-directed" personality.

There is much evidence today, however, that the 1960s and 1970s were grand experiments that failed. Divorce and separation rates soared, free sexuality proved disappointing, drug use became abusive and took the lives of some of our finest and most talented young people. Young couples grew disillusioned with living together "as if" they were married and longed for the real thing. Many observers felt that the 1960s and 1970s resulted in a loss of commitment to core values and basic institutions. At the end of the 1980s people appeared to be groping for absolutes and a renewed sense of belonging and commitment.

The 1980s (much influenced by Ronald Reagan's brand of politics and economics) promised people more concrete lives, predictability and a return to time-honored institutions and basic values. Here now was an age that promised commitment to something larger and more lasting than individual license and unbridled selfishness. But these were promises that the 1980s could not fulfill. While people groped for commitment, they found only a return to conformity; in the search for something in their lives more deep and meaningful, people discovered that, again, they had to be like everyone else. The pressures to measure up, perform and succeed had returned with a vengeance.

America today is not simply a replica or an extension of the 1950s. Political, economic, religious and educational institutions have changed too much. Continued economic prosperity is not nearly as evident or taken for granted by business leaders, and there is the well-documented shift from a production- to a service-oriented economy. The sudden popularity of patriotism, the emergence of the religious right, the "careerism" of today's high school and college student, the two-income family are among the many changes in our society that make a comparison with the 1950s very difficult.

Yet, the specter of conformity is evident again today at every turn in American culture. But this must not be understood only as a conformity that meets the demands of contemporary society. In every culture there is a certain degree of conformity. The situation in which we find ourselves now is unique to its time, but also common to all societies in varying degrees.

It is my contention that American adults, adolescents and children are finding their lives constrained, controlled and manipulated by conformity mechanisms far less visible and less direct than in earlier eras. Because the styles of conformity are less recognizable, Americans often find themselves feeling anxious and constrained without knowing the source. My goal here is to examine how these recent styles of conformity or the "unconscious" social forces are affecting the lives of contemporary men and women.

Introduction

What are the hidden forms of conformity in American culture? I would argue that they are, in part, found in the performance ethic, an ethic that forms the basis of social judgment in much, if not all, of contemporary America. Life today means having to measure up to an almost endless variety of performance standards. In all that we do, in all that we are or want to become, we are judged, measured and constantly evaluated. We must meet socially mandated standards of performance whether it is the age at which we are toilet-trained, our level of family income, or the number of dates we have as a teenager. The self that results can best be described as the "measured self."

While the performance ethic in American culture has had a long development, our purpose here is to describe and understand its consequences for today's women and men. Though I do not propose to paint a gloomy picture of our lives, we must confront the worst if we are to devise something better and see ourselves in a new light and dream of fresh possibilities of being and becoming.

Our cultural mania for measuring and evaluating people and virtually everything about them is a form of conformity and, like all forms of conformity/control, an example of tyranny. The performance ethic is not imposed or mandated by the use of decree or bayonet. Individuals are not shot for refusing to subject themselves to unremitting evaluation; they are merely encouraged to, or made to look silly or sick if they don't. Moreover, the modern performance ethic is built into the very process of socialization. That is, we learn to judge ourselves and to judge others, and we come to *want* to judge ourselves and others. Americans often find themselves comfortable in the "measured self," and find it difficult to imagine their lives working out in any other way, or to contrive other possibilities of being.

We are constantly encouraged to measure ourselves and others. We want to perform. This is what the socialization process does,

Performance Ethics in American Culture

and the culture provides all sorts of arenas in which to "prove ourselves": home, school, sports, the workplace and even the bedroom.

Like many forms of socialization, the performance ethic has become internalized. Americans now feel bad about themselves if they don't measure up; they even feel uneasy if people fail to measure them. Today, perhaps more than ever, people want what the modern culture gives — and they want it because of guilt feelings that arise if they don't go along in a genuine desire to please others. Psychologists tell us that guilt is a strong motivator; that is why it takes an extraordinary effort to reject the measured self. But guilt must be expiated. Society must offer the means of atonement. Thus public approval is the other side of the coin in the performance ethic. Americans are urged increasingly by guilt and the rewards offered to those who succeed to want to perform and be evaluated. Their guilt is atoned through public approval and material benefits and power when they measure up, meet the standard, or have satisfactory evaluations.

Much of this book is about the downside of the performance ethic. While some adults, adolescents and children enjoy the rewards of successful performance and derive much satisfaction in their pursuit of the measured self, many find neither personal satisfaction nor do they enjoy societal approval and reward. Many pay dearly when they fail to measure up or attempt to drop out of the performance culture altogether. And we cannot be blind to the human suffering produced by the performance culture any more than we can ignore the human carnage wrought by the industrial/technological culture, though the former is less well-understood and easy to recognize. But surely there is a link between our cultural mania for evaluation and measured performance and our increasing suicide rate, drug abuse problem, eating disorders among women and alcoholism among men and women. Performance anxiety is not limited to the bedroom in our

Introduction

culture. It has permeated our schools, homes, workplaces and even our leisure activities. And it is a form of performance anxiety that I feel is connected to some of the more regrettable and publicized self-destructive behaviors exhibited by adults, adolescents and children in our society.

My focus in this book confines itself to those segments of American life which seem most vulnerable to the performance ethic. Thus, I have taken a quasidevelopmental approach, examining the performance ethic through the human life cycle, from the earliest years of childhood and family life, through adolescence and ultimately through the period of what Americans now call "middle life." The developmental analysis is augmented by brief excursions into the world of sexuality and performance in the bedroom, and the meaning and consequences of the performance ethic in the American workplace. The book continues with a look at poverty and unemployment in our society, how measurement mania in the economy is producing a permanent class of people, mainly minorities, who have little chance now of "making it" economically in America. The concluding chapter offers new insights in reordering human values and priorities in America to restore a more humane individualism and a more authentic freedom of personality.

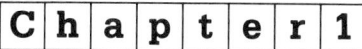

Measuring Up
The Early Years

In March, 1986, *Parents Magazine* ran a feature article by freelance writer Terry Williams, in which she asked fifty mothers what they would do differently if given another opportunity to raise their children. Here is what three of the women in her sample revealed.

- One mother of a three-year-old would have chosen only *one* child care book to follow, rather than be confused by advice given in the dozens she now owned.
- Another young mother would have switched her pediatrician more quickly, having endured his disapproval for too many years. Her present doctor thinks she is a good mother.
- Finally, a working mother of two would have made herself immune to the guilt feelings she developed when others criticized how she raised her children.

Such is the lot of all too many young mothers and even fathers in a society where the performance ethic flourishes. Raising chil-

Measuring Up

dren to succeed, achieve and "measure up" becomes fraught with self-doubts and ambiguities. Am I a good mother? A good father? Am I fit for parenting? Do I read the right child care books? Am I getting the most up-to-date expert advice? Do I listen to the right people about what I should be doing for my kids? These and similar questions point to the gnawing uncertainties that characterize modern parenting, making it the one contemporary social role that, especially for the professional, middle class of America, no one enters into lightly.

And why should this be so? Parents have raised children for thousands of years and in most times and places did what came naturally, or what was dictated by tradition, local custom, or community norms. And their children, with some exceptions, grew to adulthood according to the same traditional or community standards. Why is it that today parents are so unsure of themselves and their abilities, so fearful and anxious about how their children will "turn out," so quick to see their children as problems and so ready to seek advice from experts?

I feel that the answer to these questions lies in the way the performance ethic, the "measuring-up" process, has permeated modern American society, with its limitless demands on people of all ages and statuses to achieve, make good, count for something and to prove to themselves and others that they have what it takes to succeed. Probably the one thing that today's parents fear most is that not only might their children fail to succeed, but that they themselves, as parents, might fail to provide the firm footing, the "proper" home environment considered necessary for their children to grow and to succeed.

Our cultural mandate to succeed and prove worthy makes childhood and childrearing a difficult time for parent and child alike. And the prevailing wisdom in America maintains that the earliest years of a child's life are the most crucial for the prodding, nudging and nurturing necessary to move toward a successful and

The Early Years

and worthy life as an adolescent and adult. Woe to the parents who fail to recognize the child's achievement "gifts," or who are slow to pick up on developmental problems, or who do not provide constant attention and intensive nurturing for their offspring. And pity the poor children who fail to measure up because their parents read the wrong books, are blind to their shortcomings, are preoccupied with their own needs and desires, or who just don't have what it takes to parent for success. Indeed, family life in middle class America is not to be taken lightly today, unless, of course, Bill Cosby is the father and Phylicia Ayers-Allen is the mother.

The measuring-up process in America actually begins prior to childhood, as any good obstetrician or obstetric nurse can tell us. In a culture driven by the performance ethic even the newest born, fresh out of the womb, are not immune to its influence. One of the very first things that happens to American babies born in a hospital (and most of them are) is that they get measured. Dr. Virginia Apgar saw to that in 1952 when she developed her now famous and widely accepted Apgar Score, a numerical scale evaluating a baby's clinical vitality and well-being at the moment of birth. Heart rate, respiratory effort, muscle tone, reflex irritability (measured by thumping the bottom of the baby's foot) and color are each rated on a zero-to-three scale by a nurse trained in Apgar measurement within one to three minutes of delivery. A score in the range of seven to ten indicates a clinically healthy baby; lower scores call for immediate resuscitation procedures. Most babies fall in the upper range of scores.[1] Since American culture, in general, rewards brainy success more than brawny success (with the exception of professional athletics) obstetricians inform us, and we are pleased to learn, that Apgar scores in the seven-to-ten range correlate strongly with the absence of neurological distress at age one. In other words, most

Measuring Up

babies measuring up well on Apgar are mentally fit at the end of their first year.

I'm not arguing that Apgar measurements should not be used. I recognize that the Apgar Score serves the primary and very worthwhile purpose of identifying at the moment of birth those babies in physical distress. However, it is more than coincidental that in our culture each baby begins life measured on a one-to-ten scale. I wonder how many young parents today might be heard in the corridors of countless maternity wards, mildly boasting to their relatives and friends how well their baby did on the Apgar: "Yes, she's off to a good start." More to the point, perhaps, how many babies in our society will find their subsequent childhood, adolescence and adult years filled with numerical measurements of their character, intelligence, competence and health, all for their own good?

While it is difficult to be critical of the use of Apgar scores for newborns, isn't it also difficult to find fault with the logic and apparent benevolence of intelligence tests, personality assessments, popularity ratings, stress-level scores and myriad other measuring devices we have developed to evaluate, categorize and label people, all for their own good? There is a seductiveness about the way we value measuring people. As long as the measurements are objective and scientific, and carried out for the person's own good, they are considered benign.

But I'm getting ahead of myself. Let's return to our newborn baby and the beginning of her innocent measurements. Following the Apgar measures, nurses diligently record the infant's weight and length, and scrutinize further for any signs of abnormalities. Length and weight proportions are the more commonly familiar and publicly revealed of the baby's measurements and serve as the source of many a parent's bragging rights in the social world of the maternity ward. What proud father can be restrained from informing relatives, friends, all who will listen, and

The Early Years

some who won't, about the weight and length of his baby boy? Interestingly, many hospital maternity wards encourage this measurement passion by installing large picture windows for the nurseries where newborns can be viewed by visitors, with some hospitals providing cards attached to the cribs listing the baby's length and weight. While peering at my own infants in the maternity nursery, I found that the longest and heaviest babies drew the most admiring glances and the most sustained "ooh's" and "aah's."

This is the beginning of the measuring-up process in America: the crib, the first report card from the attending physician and nurse that the infant is initially O.K. and much can be expected. From earliest infancy through toddlerhood, the child's life will become a testing ground to assess how well the youngster will do in later life. Though the infant lying innocently and sleepily in the crib cannot know it, in those earliest days all eyes, professional, paternal and familial, which look down at the crib, scientifically and lovingly, are also peering judgmentally for signs of future potential. And it will fall upon the infant's parents not only to love, but to judge; not only to admire, but to assess; to accept some traits in their infant, but to hunt for and measure many others. And to what end? In American culture, the devotion of parents to their newborn is tempered with their desire to see in the infant something of their own dreams and aspirations, something of their own talents and achievements, something of themselves — in a word, their replica.

Americans are living in an era in which virtually everyone is expected to grow and develop according to various stages and standards. The earliest months of a toddler's life are seen as absolutely crucial in forming habits, traits and competencies that will set the tone for the child's future. The prevailing cultural wisdom in America, which for some years now has been heavily influenced by theories of developmental psychology and other

Measuring Up

scientific and quasiscientific disciplines emphasizing human development and growth, constantly reminds parents that if children fail in their initial measurements, corrections should be sought, and the sooner the better. Today's parents can draw from a bottomless well of professional advice—from child psychologists, pediatricians, psychiatrists, social workers and a host of other "experts on the child." For parents unable to pay the fees associated with private consultation, any bookstore or newsstand has a plethora of magazines, books, handbooks and manuals on childrearing, available at reasonable paperback rates.

The Serious Childhood

Are we too obsessed with our children today? And has the performance ethic which drives our culture so relentlessly taken much of the joy and spontaneity out of childhood? Have we as parents become so concerned with how our children are performing on some scale of development that we are afraid to let our children just "be" and live in the world as children? I think the answer to these questions is a resounding "yes." But, there is hope for something better. We must first identify the problem.

Historian Philip Aries, in his study *Centuries of Childhood*, discovered the truth about our modern obsession with childrearing.[2] Using historical materials and investigation, Aries found that as recently as the seventeenth century our European ancestors did not have the language to distinguish the ages of children. Nor did they have any concept or special age category denoting what we know as adolescence. The idea of an extended childhood, which is taken for granted in our thinking today, did not exist for Europeans prior to the seventeenth century. Artists, for example, merely portrayed children as miniature adults. In other words, Europeans had yet to discover childhood!

Moreover, children attended school at all ages; they started and finished pretty much as they pleased. Schools were not divided into age-grades. In fact, it was the very concept of age-grade schooling, initiated in the eighteenth and nineteenth centuries, that began to create the notion of childhood itself. Schooling created the possibilities for childhood as a special age of life. Aries also discovered that in the eighteenth century the family began to separate itself from society and community influence, and the idea of a private family life gradually emerged. Along with this came a new desire for personal isolation; individuals and family members wanted more seclusion and privacy from the communities that had dictated personal lifestyles and behaviors for centuries. Families built houses featuring separate rooms, a personal bedroom or sitting room for example, where individuals could be alone and feel a sense of privacy.

All of this starts to sound very modern (only about 200 years ago) and familiar to us, and who can argue with the need for privacy and a chance to be alone? Aries contends that as family life became more private, parents grew increasingly concerned with the health of their children, which they tended to connect with the child's progress. Even more importantly, parents began to see education as necessary for their children; schooling would help their children progress in a healthy way. Parents got ample support in their ideas from religious moralists who taught that it was the parents' duty to start their children to school in early life. Thus, the child was removed from adult society. According to Aries, from the eighteenth century on, children were no longer *free*; they were constrained and controlled by the authority of the church, school and family. The resulting situation caused Aries to lament, "Our world is obsessed by the physical, moral, and sexual problems of childhood."[3]

In the space of a few hundred years the idea of childhood took shape, and in many ways this was a remarkable achievement. Since children were no longer considered miniature adults, they

Measuring Up

were given a special place in the world and there are, no doubt, many positive aspects of an extended childhood. Children are no longer physically mutilated or branded for committing crimes; they are no longer made to work endless hours in unsafe and unhealthy sweat-shops; they are not apprenticed out to work for other families and treated as servants. We have made noteworthy advances in the quality of life for our children.

However, there is another side of the coin that must be faced squarely if we are to create a better world for parents and children, and herein lies the problem. In the process of establishing a special age of life called childhood, we run the risk of becoming obsessed with our children and their progress. If the typical parents in sixteenth-century Europe cared too little about their child's development, we are equally guilty of caring too much. And if the child living 400 years ago had too much freedom and too few expectations, children in our world aren't free enough, and have far too much pressure.

There exists a seriousness about childhood in our culture that, if not deadly, is certainly stultifying and constraining for both child and parent. Once the idea of childhood developed in Western societies, it became vulnerable to all the pressures of the performance ethic. Children are pressured to define their selfhood in terms of how well they perform at school, at play and during their earliest years in accomplishing developmental tasks.

When parents in America bring home their newborn from the hospital, they soon feel the weighty pressure of what is considered to be the monumental task of raising their child properly. Given the infusion of the performance ethic in our culture and urged on by the tenets of developmental psychology, parents are expected to see to it that their children form all the habits, attitudes, abilities and personality configurations that will allow them to grow and progress to a successful future. Parents are admonished to avoid serious mistakes in childrearing during these earliest

The Early Years

months and years, lest the child be irreversibly damaged and marked for failure. Today's parent is not so much expected to be a taskmaster as a "child developer," and the sooner parents see themselves as amateur psychologists the better. Any mom who thumbs her nose at modern psychology is not fit to be a parent in today's world, as any woman's magazine on the supermarket shelf can attest.

The curious reader might ask where these ideas about parent-as-psychologist came from, and the answer is provided by author David Elkind. In his book *The Hurried Child*, Elkind traces the tremendous boom in child development to a period in America shortly after the Second World War.[4] Elkind notes that prior to the war there were only two professional journals devoted to child development. Within a few decades of the war there were, and are, more than a dozen! In the soil of prosperity that followed World War II, with an expanding American middle class and the emergence of the white-collar suburb, child development theory and popular psychology found fertile ground. Parenting in America took a new direction that, with some modifications, remains the same today. Parenting became wedded to child development, the service being performed by priestly psychologists in the Home of Reason.

I'm not being facetious here (well, maybe a little). Only a century or two ago, the moral authority over children rested upon the triumvirate of the church, school and family. Eventually, as societies secularized, as the institution of the church diminished as a moral force in controlling attitudes and behaviors, the school and family had to go it alone in shaping the lives of children. However, with the discovery that children can "develop," child-rearing in America soon became a professional province for developmental psychologists. In many respects, and at the risk of oversimplifying, modern psychology has replaced the church in America, partly as a moral force, but even more as a definer of reality about children, what they are like and how they should be raised.

David Elkind does not underestimate the valuable contributions made by child development theory, but he does lament that today's parents want to "hurry" their children along the developmental path too quickly. Thus, our children now feel pressured to mature and solve developmental tasks sooner than they are actually capable; they feel compelled to accomplish things they aren't competent to do. If this continues, Elkind argues, we are in danger of losing our sense of childhood in America.

There is much truth in what Elkind says, but I feel he has not identified *why* parents feel constrained to put so much pressure on their children. I think the reason is that parents themselves are under enormous pressure to parent for success. If childhood has become overly serious, so has parenting in modern America, and it is due in considerable part to the performance ethic. Since our expectation is that children become or "develop" into successful adults, it is absolutely essential in our society that children get off on the right foot, and it is the parents' duty to insure that their child's progress toward the various rewards of later life is accurately assessed and measured.

The seriousness of childhood in America begins with the parents' compulsive preoccupation with their toddler's basic competencies and acquired human characteristics, such as walking, talking and toilet-training. The ages at which these abilities are mastered have become cultural mandates and the source of much parental anxiety. A child's inability to acquire these competencies at a certain point on the developmental timetable was taken for a decade or two in America as an indication of backwardness, or status as a slow learner. Parents fretted over a child's lack of "progress" because they feared their child wasn't as bright as other children, and hence behind on the track for future success. Fortunately, current child development theory has relaxed and liber-

The Early Years

alized many of these rigid norms, and, in fact, today's parents are informed by some groups of experts that each child should develop its own timetable. Children must not be pushed too hard, but they should develop. The "new" developmental psychology, with its more flexible notions of developmental timetables, still doesn't relieve all parents of anxiety over their children's progress, as we learn from Jean Marzollo.

Marzollo, writing in June 1985 for *Parents Magazine*, argues in Elkind-like fashion that our children are growing up too fast. As a mother Marzollo felt the pressure to see to it that her own children were early developers and were hurried along the road to maturity. Concerned about her children's eventual success, she fretted a good deal over the early toilet-training of her toddlers and whether they developed reading skills at an early age. Like many mothers she read books for advice and, particularly, had relied on *How to Multiply Your Baby's Intelligence* by Glen Doman and *The First Three Years of Life* by Burton White.[5] Marzollo eventually discovered that experts like Doman and White tried to make parents feel guilty if their children don't get pushed early and often in getting a good start in life. White's book, for example, gives young parents the dire warning that the first three years of life "fix" the child's fate for future accomplishment.

Jean Marzollo did indeed feel guilty after reading such books and wondered whether she was doing the best for her children. She assuaged her guilt, however, in the one manner so common to many middle-class parents today: she read another book prepared by experts, whose advice more nearly matched her own motherly instincts and inclinations. This book, *Child Behavior* by Frances Ilg, Louise Bates and Sidney Baker, was based on concepts derived from research conducted at the Gesell Institute for Human Development.[6] These experts argued that children develop according to "natural" stages, and that early parental prodding and pushing was neither necessary nor helpful. In other words, let nature take its course. This advice proved music to Jean Marzollo's ears. She was greatly relieved to learn that her own children were normal, but she required her own school of experts to provide her with some peace of mind.

The plight of Jean Marzollo reminds us of the tremendous ambivalence faced by men and women today as they try to parent for success. If I am going to measure up as a parent in raising my children, which school of psychological experts do I turn to for the "correct" approach? What role should I play and how vigorously should I play it in helping my child develop? Can I feel comfortable and assured as a parent playing a passive role, letting my children grow up naturally, when one psychologist says "yes," another "no," and another "maybe"?

If, as a parent, I read Jean Marzollo's article in *Parents Magazine*, I might be relieved to learn my children aren't doomed if they aren't reading or toilet-trained by a certain age. I'll be a follower of Marzollo and let my kids develop according to nature's way. Yet, if I had also read an article in the January 1985 issue of *Parents*, I would learn that seven is the perfect age. According to this article, seven is the age at which developmental tasks come together and children get the most out of formal instruction in school. Now if I have a seven-year-old who isn't doing so well in school, or is causing problems around the house, will reading this second article provide help or cause anxiety? And who is right anyway? If children develop according to nature's plan, why should nature favor age seven, and why is my child so unnatural for a seven-year-old?

Such are the joys and anxieties of parenting in the age of the expert and in a culture dominated by the performance ethic: where does one turn for the best advice, and who does one blame when children fail to measure up? As Philip Aries discovered, childhood in modern life is indeed an age "set apart," yet a period in which the children must develop and show what they are made

The Early Years

of. Parents too must test their mettle in proving to themselves and others that they have what it takes to mold and shape their offspring in a successful direction.

Not only is childhood a special age, but increasingly one set off as an early warning period for future achievement or potential failure. David Elkind contends that childhood is now becoming less valued as a life of its own, but more as a period in which a youngster's future abilities are tested and assessed. Parents and other adult authorities are under a cultural mandate to detect the best in children as well as the worst. Just as all children carry the potential for their future achievements and accomplishments, likewise they sow the seeds of their own failures. And these potentials and liabilities are, in turn, thought to be nurtured and pruned by parental role models. Correct parenting nurtures success; improper parenting can produce deviants. It is increasingly accepted that the best in children is the result of good parenting, while the worst in children lies in parental failure. Given the professional language and ideology of child development, the early warning signs of a child's potential are recognizable, predictable and correctable, and it is the parents' role to accomplish all three.

Two examples stand out where parents are especially anxious, and vulnerable to the charge that they failed their children through their own faulty parenting: juvenile delinquency and homosexuality.

Americans have a love-hate relationship with juvenile delinquency. On the one hand, we romanticize the delinquent as a rebel, with or without a cause, in popular movies, novels and television shows. Yet we also abhor delinquency, and at various times in our history have regarded it as one of our most pressing social problems. More current public thinking connects delinquency to our national decline in economic productivity, the general cultural malaise and forms of behavior such as drug abuse and sexual promiscuity. In accounting for the pervasiveness of delinquency, both professional judgment and lay opinion place the blame at the doorstep of the home and family; that is to say, the parents of the delinquent are considered the real failures. Since the 1950s the familiar saying, "There is no such thing as a bad child, only bad parents," has become almost axiomatic in our culture.

Journalist and author Howard James' book *Children in Trouble* is representative of the way in which delinquency was explained and understood for several decades in America.[7] James devotes an entire chapter to "How Parents Produce Delinquents," as if the process were similar to the way General Motors produces Camaros. James contends that the many teachers, social workers, probation officers and reform-school administrators he talked to all agreed that parents should be the ones sent to jail rather than the children. He goes on to list twenty-two reasons why parents fail their children and produce delinquents. Among them are: parental immaturity, TV addicted parents and parents who neglect to build their child's self-confidence.

Given books such as this, and countless magazine articles, television documentaries and government reports, is it any wonder that parents pressure their children to hurry through childhood and master developmental tasks? The sooner the child gets beyond the legal-age limit of delinquency the better; then when things go wrong, it is someone else's fault and mom and dad are off the hook.

The other fear characterizing modern parenting is that one's child will fail in proper sex role socialization and become homosexual. Perhaps for some parents this is the ultimate fear, given that the social stigma of homosexuality is so severe in our culture. Moreover, as Letty Pogrebin, author of *Feminist Frontiers: Rethinking Sex, Gender and Society*, points out, the fear remains hidden and unspoken, yet is real enough to prevent parents from

The Early Years

letting their children be truly free.[8] Pogrebin shows us that parental fear grows out of a specific cultural conditioning emphasizing that sex roles produce sexuality and that certain ingredients create homosexuality in children. For example, if boys are raised to be real men, acting masculine, brave and tough, they won't become homosexual. The ingredients assumption also contends that certain features of the child—hormones, for example—or early family environment predispose him to homosexuality. Psychoanalytic theory is one of the ingredients assumptions holding the family responsible for homosexuality. As the argument goes, it is the family's duty to teach children proper sex-role behavior, so there won't be any mix-ups in sex identity. If a child becomes homosexual it is due to the family's failure in teaching sex roles, in much the same way that family neglect or parental TV addiction leads to delinquency.

We can credit Letty Pogrebin for dispelling these dangerous assumptions, for she has amply demonstrated that there is little, if any, scientific evidence linking homosexuality to sex-role socialization or to a specific ingredient. No one knows for sure what causes or produces homosexuality. Yet these fears persist in our society because we have so little tolerance for homosexuality. As long as we feel homosexuality is one of the worst things that can happen to our offspring, neither parent nor child will be free to play their roles as they would like.

Intensive Parenting

In recent years, "parenting for success" has come to mean intensive and constant parenting. The new ideology, and one quite consistent with developmental child psychology, decrees that children will acquire attributes and traits necessary for success if parents are constant and intensive nurturers, supporters, morale-builders and role models. What boy will learn to

Measuring Up

compete today if his dad won't take part in Little League? And no mom is worthy of the name if she isn't willing to sit behind the wheel of the family's Toyota van for hours driving her children from one lesson or day camp to another. The performance ethic in our culture has made it almost mandatory that parents learn to drive, for how else are children going to get to all the lessons so critical in their developmental growth? To say that children are driven in our society is both figurative and literal.

The fascinating aspect of intensive parenting is that it comes at a point when the divorce rate has increased the number of single-parent families, and economic insecurities have made the two-income family necessary and commonplace. As parents have less time available for their children due to economic responsibilities, the emerging cultural expectation is that parenting should be intensive, constant and extremely attentive. Especially among middle-class parents, there is unremitting pressure to keep their children occupied with structured activities and recreation that will bring out the "best" in them. The Organizational Man who was the representative figure of the 1950s has been replaced by the Organizational Child of the 1980s. Permit me to use a personal example to illustrate this.

As a college professor, I reside in a relatively small, quiet Midwestern community where I have had much contact with parents of school-age children. In the past several years, as I have casually observed family life in my community, I've been impressed with the fact that children of middle-class parents rarely appear to have any free time. Even their leisure, recreational and supposedly "fun" activities are highly organized and tightly scheduled, and their parents seem to prefer it this way.

I'm sensitive about this because I recall my childhood as being much different. I grew up in the late 1940s and 1950s in a working-class suburb on Chicago's West Side. Our brick streets and vacant lots were always filled with young boys playing ball,

The Early Years

and girls jumping rope, and there were rarely any adults around. This didn't seem to bother us any. Our parents often reminded us that they were too busy to "watch us play," and we got used to it, and enjoyed the freedom that came with being left alone. When we played baseball in the streets, we provided our own equipment, we chose our own sides, enforced our own rules. In short, our "play" was pretty much up to us. While we might have lacked some adult approval by being left to our own devices, we escaped their censure and disappointment as well. Things have changed.

Today when I inquire about the summer plans of my colleagues at the university where I teach, so many of them describe itineraries revolving around their children's organized activities. Little League, soccer, tennis and swim-team coaching will occupy the men, while their spouses and my female colleagues will take their children traveling, to music lessons, ballet lessons, day camps, etc. Almost every parent I know tries to see that their children take enough lessons to become proficient at something. Perhaps another Virginia Wade, Jimmy Connors, Pele or Stan Musial? No middle-class child in my community can grow to maturity without taking lessons, attending camps and being part of at least three organized groups, such as 4-H, Boy Scouts, DeMolay, Brownies, to say nothing of time spent in the dentist's chair having braces adjusted. All of these groups and activities depend on parents becoming highly involved as boosters, volunteer coaches, morale-builders and, most importantly, as uncomplaining chauffeurs. If there is ever another oil embargo, childhood will cease to exist in Middle America.

Few parents refuse to become involved because they want so badly for their children to succeed in life, and they view these activities as terribly instrumental in their child's development for success. For middle-class parents today, this is a large part of what it means to do "right" by your children.

Pre-adolescent youth especially find their lives structured

around lessons, sports instruction and organized leisure. In my community it is now fashionable for university faculty to sponsor day camps during the summer using university facilities. In the past, most of these camps were strictly athletic (tennis, basketball, etc.), but for the last few summers athletic instruction has been combined with courses in computer instruction. A ten-year-old now can go to "camp" for two weeks, learn to dribble in the morning and to program in the afternoon. Middle-class parents in this community find the combination of computer literacy and the competitive ethic appealing. Thus, summer camps for children are no longer merely for fun, but now have a competitive seriousness about them. Children are being prepared to succeed in the middle-class arenas they will join as adults. After all, what child can perform well in the world without being computer literate and having a good backhand? For the middle-class ten-year-old, the micro-chip has replaced the chocolate chip as the core of passion.

I can see emerging in middle-class America today a new *Parkinson's Law of Parenting*: mom and dad (or the single parent) must see to it that organized activity expands to fill a child's every available minute. This is why parents so willingly accept the authority of the public schools. They know the child's day is organized around a balance of task-oriented and expressive activities, and parents feel that this will help their children "grow." And once school is finished, for the day or the summer, parents are quick to structure their child's activities as they feverishly search for groups and programs that will assist in their child's development. For parents, the implicit function of organized sports, instructional camps and endless lessons is that such activities promote "growth," and without growth there can be no success.

Feminist writer Barbara Ehrenreich, in her book *The Hearts of Men*, traces the ethic of growth in American culture to the 1960s, when American psychology shifted its view of human nature.[9]

The Early Years

For a number of years psychologists defined personal maturity as the end-state of a long series of developmental tasks. In the sixties they redefined maturity as an accumulation of "growth experiences." According to Ehrenreich, psychologists encouraged people to look at life as an adventure, and to see that human potential was unlimited. Moreover, people had a responsibility, if they were to tap their potential, to move from one peak experience to another in the search for the actualized self. Individuals were not only free to grow but under a cultural mandate to do so. Psychological growth soon became one of the new measuring rods of the sixties and seventies—how much are you growing in relation to others? How much of your human potential have you tapped?

I think it is fairly easy to see how today's parents cling to the notion of growth and want to give their children as many opportunities as possible to unleash their unlimited potential. Whether these parents feel they have tapped all of their own potential, or whether they have had all the self-actualization they want or can stand, they must certainly feel an obligation to give their children the opportunity. And if their child complains or resists, parents need only remind her that signing up for computer camp is for her own good. How else to discover your potential as a systems analyst? How else will you master your ground strokes?

Organized sports, instructional camps and the endless round of lessons have an underlying seriousness about them that I feel many children sense but cannot articulate because they lack the language of protest. The Parkinson's Law of Parenting, which drives children into an increasingly organized and structured life, serves to heighten the measuring-up process for children and the pressure they must certainly feel. Whether on the Little League field or at the piano recital, children find that their fun activities are another context in which they are tested, probed, expected to "look good," and show potential for even greater future accomplishment. And not only this, but they must accept the rationale

Measuring Up

that their physical and mental health depends on it, and that they owe it to themselves, their parents, and others to grow and develop their potentials. As children they must realize that they can never merely content themselves with being; they must see their lives as becoming, an unfolding process of growth experiences that never really end. The performance ethic for America's children means that today's accomplishments are never taken as ends in themselves, but only as signposts for potential and growth.

I agree with David Elkind that we are robbing children of whatever joy there is in childhood by hurrying them through it and pushing too hard. But the problem lies deeper than that. Our children are under too much pressure to perform. We are creating situations, for example, where a child will feel she is a failure if she's not computer literate at age ten! Every child's organized activity creates an occasion for failure as well as success, feelings of inadequacy as well as achievement. Even more insidious and damaging to children than this, however, is that we have allowed much of the psychology of growth and the human potential movement, as ideologies, to color our view of childhood. If children are bundles of potential, and if their potentials are unlimited, no childhood accomplishment is of intrinsic value anymore. Nothing a child does can please himself or his parents except as potential, an indication only that future accomplishments will be forthcoming, and even these will pale in comparison to the ones that will follow. Such a situation can only heighten the pressures and ambiguities of childhood and parenting alike.

Today's children are not only vulnerable to the stresses of the performance ethic, as they define their identities in terms of their ability to measure up, but they also develop ambivalent attitudes toward their parents. Children desire, long for and need the nurturing love and intimacy of their parents. They seek uncondi-

The Early Years

tional and unqualified parental love. Yet, in our culture as they move through childhood, they also seek their parents' approval in performance-related activities. Children want their parents to think they are doing well, whether it is in school, at camp, in recital or on the Little League field.

To a certain degree, this has always been so. I can remember, as a boy on the streets near Chicago, we always liked it if our parents would take time to watch us play for a while, and we could show off a little. And, of course, a good report card was valued as a way of seeking approval. Yet, that was an era before Little League, as an organized arena of competitive pressure, was fully developed and accepted in suburban culture. And our fathers were not coaches! (The fathers of boys in my neighborhood were working double shifts in local factories.) And we were advised to do well in school, not so much as a sign of our potential (though I had a few teachers who employed this language), but because it was an expectation. The 1950s, as Ehrenreich and others have noted, was an age of conformity, and decent grades in school were an indication of conformity, following the rules and a matter of duty and respect toward parents. In other words, I think there was a greater consistency between what we as children felt our parents expected of us and what we felt we could deliver.

I'm not sure this is the case today. For good grades and occasional "showing off" today are not valued as ends, but only as growth-enhancing performances and signs of potential for future accomplishments. Hence the greater ambivalence our children must feel, when their parents' love is always mixed with their desire to see their child grow and actualize. The latter are accomplishments not only difficult to assess (though psychologists certainly try) and live up to, but limitless and unending. Children fear that if they don't live up to their potential, they forfeit not only their parents' approval but their love as well. While I've

Measuring Up

stated that this problem is generic to all parent-child relationships in America, the problem seems especially acute today, and I would like to examine Little League activities as a case in point.

To return to my neighborhood in the 1950s, as boys we played a lot of baseball, but few of us were involved in Little League because the concept was so new it was just beginning to be popular. Our baseball was played on sandlots and in streets, and adults were rarely connected to our games. If my father ever watched me play, it was only briefly, and while I sought to look good when he watched, I was not bothered by my poor play. We were both accustomed to it. More importantly, in that era street baseball was mostly *play*. While each team tried to win, it was no shame to lose or to look bad doing so. (Besides, if your team lost you could always defend yourself by declaring that the sides were uneven.)

Youth baseball changed from child's play to a serious game in America with the advent of Little League, and it was usurped by grown men. In the quiet, college community where I now live Little League is serious business, and the point of each game is not only to win but to look good in the process. The only boys invited to play are those that show potential for high-caliber baseball skills. There are major leagues and minor leagues and even a competitive draft system. More significantly, teams are coached by fathers of the players, and some boys find themselves coached by their *own* fathers. A few of my university colleagues have coached their own sons (while I have assisted) and the pressure on the field and in the dug-out was at times thick enough to cut with a knife. These coaches were well-intentioned, well-meaning fathers, and bright, sensitive and caring men. But often I saw their sons leave the pitching mound with tears in their eyes. And though the fathers didn't verbalize or convey their disappointment or disapproval, their sons no doubt felt it. They sensed they were letting down their father-as-coach by pitching poorly. These

The Early Years

were awkward and trying moments for fathers and sons alike, both victims not only of Little League but the pressure of the performance ethic in American culture.

The father-as-coach phenomenon I feel is the prototype of the parent-child pressures youngsters experience in their overly-organized lives. The child of the 1950s, awkwardly and eagerly showing off for his parents at play, has been replaced by the child of the 1980s, all too pressured to look good, perform well, show potential. And as parents are required to assume the more formal roles of coach, leader, director, etc. of their children's organized growth activities this problem can only deepen. And I'm not referring here only to the pressures generated in a highly competitive society, but the more pervasive and less-well-understood demands placed on people for evaluation and approval. Children can often avoid the risk of competitive situations, but today they can rarely avoid the evaluative and judgmental context necessitated by the performance ethic. Thus our children are often torn between their needs for the unqualified love and acceptance of their parents, and their conditioned desire to measure up, grow and actualize in ways that will gain their parents' approval.

Parents and Guilt

Today's parents, whether single or married, are also facing new pressures to perform well as parents. Under current conditions fathers and mothers can no longer content themselves with providing materially for their children within a family context of love. In the present what constitutes good parenting is varied and multifaceted, and depends on what books are read, psychologists consulted or television programs and commercials watched. As I have described earlier, one effect of the performance ethic is that parents are expected to structure their children's lives so that the opportunities for growth, fulfillment and actualizing abound, and children can demonstrate abilities and competencies for present and future accomplishment. This mandate alone keeps many parents enormously busy.

The requirements of family life must be balanced carefully with the demands of economic livelihood for most families today, and parents are subject to considerable guilt if they feel the balance is swinging too heavily in either direction. If we look at demographics we find that: as of 1985, some fifty-six percent of families in our society had more than one earner; of married women with preschoolers, fifty-two percent were in the labor force; and over seventy percent of employed mothers were working full-time. All the while, the performance culture encourages intensive parenting.

Demographer Brad Edmundson tells us that Madison Avenue is well aware of the guilt feelings modern parents experience when trying to juggle economic and family roles.[10] Accordingly, television commercials play upon these guilt feelings in promoting products or services that in various ways help parents assuage their guilt. Xerox commercials are a prime example. In one oft-repeated commercial, Xerox office equipment is advertised as a new method of efficiently organizing a father's office, so he has time now to attend his daughter's birthday party. Dad can now be efficient and fatherly at the same time, a combination and balance so eagerly sought by young parents. Edmundson contends that parents are an "emotionally vulnerable market."[11] Their vulnerability stems from a double-bind: their desire to be economically successful and productive, and their desire to be good parents to their children. In Edmundson's words, "Children... are the bait and the emotional hook is guilt."[12]

Corollary with this idea is the emerging parental mandate to spend "quality time" with their children. We hear a good deal of talk about quality today, especially in economic/industrial circles, where, for instance, the Japanese are supposed to have

The Early Years

discovered something the United States misplaced several decades ago. Lee Iacocca fills the television airways with commercials showing him thumping the fenders of Plymouths, shouting how Chrysler Corporation has rediscovered quality and smiling broadly because the fenders, despite his thumping, remain securely fastened. As American industry searches for product quality, American parents are under a similar obligation to seek quality relationships with their children, as if anyone knew what that meant. Young fathers and mothers now worry whether their parenting skills measure up in quality, while corporations and Madison Avenue stand ready to create and promote products that will help parents out of their dilemma. Edmundson cites food companies that now promise anxious mothers nutritious foods, quick and easy to prepare, so that mom has more time for her children. United Brands, Inc. features a commercial depicting a father and son playing soccer together while eating bananas (no easy feat). The accompanying ad copy stresses that quality time goes hand-in-hand with quality food. And finally, insurance companies now play on a guilt theme of child neglect by parents being under-insured, and thus incapable of living up to commitments.

All of this points to the conclusion that parenting is no longer a natural or traditionally defined and accepted role. Parents are expected to measure up to often impossible, contradictory and nearly self-defeating standards of accomplishment. Torn between cultural demands to be economically successful and good family providers and the mandates of the new psychology of growth to be child "developers," thus ever alert and sensitive to their children's need for quality time and actualizing experiences, parents are now vulnerable to the guilt that arises when, by trying to do both, they may fail in either. And in the background and foreground of their daily rounds reverberates the reassuring commercial message that by purchasing a particular product, parents can have and do it all. To have is to do. Good parenting is the result of smart spending habits. A wise parent is an astute shopper. When David Elkind concluded that today's parents are "stressed out," is it any wonder?

Professional Mothering

Though American fathers are expected more and more to take an active role in the daily care and parenting of children, the fact remains that the mothering role is still considered most crucial in the rearing of successful children. Most of the parental pressure falls on the woman, and it is the American mother, especially the working mother, who is subject to the severest and most enduring of the guilt trips. While a significant proportion of today's mothers work full-time, the idea that mothering is a profession and women's highest calling dates back to a period in our history when far fewer mothers worked, and were relatively freer to pursue their "call."

Feminist scholars Barbara Ehrenreich and Deirdre English have fully documented the development of the mothering role in American culture with the publication of their book *For Her Own Good*.[13] The turn of the twentieth century brought a scientific approach to childrearing, at a time in American culture that childhood itself began to stand out as a distinctive time of life. Gradually children were regarded as the key to America's future, and with that idea emerged a view that children were pliant and teachable. The "noble calling" of womanhood at that time (and it persists in modified form to the present) was to raise and mold children capable of assuring America's future. As everything else in life was becoming scientific, so was motherhood; women were to rear their children properly, carefully, rationally, according to the principles of science in general and the nascent psychological sciences in particular.

Women were admonished to follow expert advice in rearing

The Early Years

their children for success. Ehrenreich and English demonstrate that every few decades the psychological scientists shifted their views of childhood and child raising; mothers, in turn, were expected to adapt with corresponding changes in their mothering approaches and relationships to their children. What was considered scientifically acceptable and successful mothering in the 1920s would have been entirely out of place in the 1950s. And by the 1960s and 1970s, women were confused by the contradictions and vacillations in psychological science. They began to distrust the advice of their child-care experts. But while they might have longed to follow their own inclinations and personal judgments, young mothers never completely gave up their reliance on experts, and to this day, women feel pressured to accept scientific advice in matters of childrearing.

Have parents, and especially mothers, lost confidence in their natural parenting abilities? Historian Christopher Lasch thinks so, and he contends that the vast amount of psychiatric and psychological advice available has not only undermined the confidence of parents, but, more importantly perhaps, has inflated the idea of the importance of childrearing techniques and parents' responsibility for failure.[14] Lasch is convincing when he says that parents today have few standards of their own for raising children, and are left with only the children's peers as measures of their child's academic and psychological development. Just as industrialization undermined and devalued the knowledge of craftsmen and workers in favor of the "scientific management" of the 1920s and 1930s, so were parental knowledge and ability devalued and made to appear unsophisticated with the rise of the psychological sciences of child development. Ehrenreich and English would concur, but they contend that mothers caught the brunt of this; their natural abilities to rear children were seen as inferior compared to the knowledge of the psychologist-expert. Moreover, the domination of the psychological sciences over mothering was but one episode in a long history of men using medical/scientific ideology to maintain their control over women in general.

Women are under considerable pressure to mother intensely so that their children can achieve and measure up, even as their natural abilities to mother are held suspect and devalued. They are subject to performance standards of good mothering against which they must measure up or fail themselves and their children. And women cannot seek a remedy to this quandary by looking within themselves, toward their own inner qualities and strengths. Like their counterparts of decades ago, they are encouraged to place their destinies as mothers in the hands of the helping professional.

Anthropologist Sheila Kitzinger uncovered a revealing contrast between mothering in American culture and mothering in peasant cultures.[15] In a peasant community there are norms of mothering that remain unquestioned, and women do not feel subject to criticism; they just do what the other women of the village have always done. By comparison, in our culture new mothers are bombarded by advice, from those who have had children and those who have not. Only in cultures such as ours, where conflicting advice abounds and women are mandated to seek it, can mothers experience failure in measuring up to motherhood norms. And only here do mothers anxiously "compare their products" to see if their child is keeping pace with the progress of other babies.[16]

Parents Magazine, which in 1977 boasted a paid circulation of 1,500,000, is typical of an American magazine for parents (but one, I suspect, that is mostly read by women), that teems with expert advice about rearing children. While it would have little value for women in peasant societies, it is eagerly read by many American women pressured to do things right as mothers. *Parents* leaves no child-rearing stone unturned; it is replete with expert/

The Early Years

scientific knowledge in the form of question and answer columns, guest articles and feature stories. For the past several years, and in keeping with the model of child development, *Parents* has contained an entire section, entitled "See How They Grow," in which the developmental stages are demarcated — "As They Grow: Birth to One Year," "As They Grow: One Year Old," etc. Each year of development is considered problematic, and thus there is a child-care expert (usually a psychologist, pediatrician or psychiatrist) who solves for the reading mother some problem she presumably will have with her offspring at that age. The anxious mother of a two-year-old can find relief by consulting the column monthly to stay on top of any difficulty she may perceive in her child or, just as likely, be alerted to problems she had not even anticipated.

School: Beyond Toddlerhood

In American culture the continuity of the measuring-up process for children and parents is assured by the public school system. In no arena is the performance ethic pursued with as much single-minded and vigorous commitment as in the school. Living up to adult expectations on the Little League field is nothing compared to the pressures in the classroom as most nine- and ten-year-olds soon discover.

As children leave the home for school, parents are relieved somewhat of the constant vigilance in seeing that their children perform up to standards, although as we shall see, momentarily parents are expected to assume an active interest in their child's school success and activities. Nevertheless, when the five-year-old enters kindergarten, his teacher will gradually become the surrogate parent, and will take on increasing responsibility in upholding performance standards. The torch is now passed to the teacher to prod, poke, size up, measure and see to it that their

Measuring Up

children "succeed." And schools armed with a host of tests and other measuring rods are more than adequately prepared for the task.

One of the underlying assumptions made by school authorities, particularly in the early primary grades, is that the child's transition from home to school will proceed smoothly if mother has done her job in the home. By this I mean, *if* the mother has intensely nurtured and prepared her children for school discipline and success by reading to them and in other ways priming the child's abilities and potentials as a kindergarten or first-grade student. While the parents are not expected to present a finished product to the teacher, they should have provided a home environment conducive to school success and inculcated values in the child that will make her teachable and competitive. Today in many public school systems, this is the least of parents' expectations.

To insure these smooth transitions and mother's continued support of and involvement with measuring-up experiences, mothers are co-opted into PTA activities. At least that was the minimum requirement of a generation or two ago. Today, even working mothers of school children are urged and cajoled into accepting roles as parent-sponsors of Brownies, Scouts and a number of booster organizations, from varsity athletics to band and choir. How many mothers of school children feel guilty when they must side-step running for PTA office because work and other commitments simply prevent them from having the time? And how much stronger the guilt feelings when these same mothers realize that many of the women who do volunteer for PTA office are just as busy and pressured as they?

One of the best pictures we have of this uneasy and sometimes anxious relationship between parents, children and schools is presented in *Crestwood Heights* by John Seeley and his colleagues.[17] Here is a remarkable study, and I recommend it for

The Early Years

anyone interested in the social life of a middle-class suburb. Though the research was carried out in Canada during the late 1950s, it sounds and feels very modern and close to home. Crestwood Heights (a fictitious name for a real community) was typical of the white-collar suburbs that sprang up throughout Canada and the United States during the economic expansion and prosperity of the 1950s. Seeley and his associates discovered that Crestwood Heights was populated by young upwardly-mobile couples and parents who pursued the "good life": success, status, material wealth not only to satisfy themselves but to set a good example for their children. The public school system in their community was considered a crucial institution because school success was virtually required for upward economic mobility and career achievement. In Crestwood Heights there was an understood connection between good parenting and a good school system; community norms encouraged, if not required, the linkage. Parents were tied to the interests of the school system through the Home and School Association, a parent-school organization that was structured to keep open the channels of communication between parents and school authorities. Mothers especially were expected to be active in the Home and School Association. A "good mother" was one who took a vital interest in her child's school life.

The two dominant values of Crestwood Heights were maturity and success, and these values permeated not only the school system. They formed the ethos of the Home and School Association as well. What this meant was that school children were encouraged to be competitive (thus successful), yet cooperative and democratic in social relationships (as a sign of maturity). During Home and School Association meetings parent interest was strongest in determining how well their own children were living up to the maturity and success values, particularly in relation to other children of similar age and grade. Parents were

Measuring Up

always pleased to learn that the school authorities shared similar concern about how students were measuring up and could provide a variety of ways to assess performance.

What was the effect of this on children? A good deal of pressure—and there was the rub. Crestwood Heights' children were expected to live up to the contradictory features of the community culture. Especially in school, children were to be success-oriented, striving for material wealth and high social status: *competitive, yet cooperative!* And a further contradiction—children were to gain a sense of maturity, the values of which were expressed in various kinds of permissiveness. School authorities promoted the idea that children needed certain "freedoms" to make their own choices in life, for the essence of maturity was a person who wisely exercised options. Yet children in Crestwood Heights were heavily imbued with success values that required them to select those options that would maximize academic-vocational achievements. What posed as freedom for children was in reality a system of forced choices, selecting among competitive means to insure eventual adult success.

Though the Home and School Association stressed a cooperative and mutually beneficial relationship between parents and school officials, Seeley's group concluded that the school was taking over more of the responsibility of childhood socialization, and, unlike many parents, was *much* more certain of its methods. For example, at Home and School meetings parents often asked for teachers' advice about rearing their children, to the point of asking what time their children should go to bed. Seeley discovers the school looming ever larger in the lives of children, with parents assuming the role of junior partners in preparing children for adult success.

Sound familiar? Has the situation changed that much in twenty-five years? Not really, if we can believe a recent (1986) *New York Times News Service* article about schools in Weston,

The Early Years

Connecticut.[18] The story is about schools in affluent Connecticut communities that are assuming increasing responsibility in "shaping the social, moral, and psychological development of their students." School officials interviewed agreed that families are less stable, and, in light of the decreasing influence of the church, schools now have to address a broad range of issues affecting the lives of school children. What the parents cannot or will not try to accomplish with their children, the schools will. School influence is becoming especially noticeable in areas of moral conduct—drinking, drug use and sexuality—areas traditionally viewed as the responsibility of family and church.

Let's take a closer look at the primary-grade teacher and his little charges. An interesting, though not unexpected, feature of education today, particularly at the primary level, is the infusion of the psychological sciences in education pedagogy. What the developmental psychologist does for young parents in our society, the educational psychologist does for teachers. Just as modern men and women find it a cultural imperative to rely heavily on expert psychological advice as parents, so do teachers find it a professional mandate to depend on psychological theories and tests in order to teach. For instance, at my university students majoring in elementary education are required to take two courses in psychology with two additional psychology courses as strongly recommended electives. No teacher in our society today is considered credible unless she is fully imbued with psychological theory, especially the models and concepts that emerge in a steady stream from educational psychology and child development. If a young man isn't comfortable seeing himself as an applied psychologist, he is hardly fit to teach.

Like most social and behavioral sciences, psychology has gained its academic prestige and cultural popularity through its ability to measure things. Whatever the human trait, skill, yearning or yen, you name it, and some psychologist can measure and

Measuring Up

test for it. And not only that, she can tell you how you rank in relation to others. Psychology has become the preeminent behavioral science in academic and popular culture because in a performance-dominated society, psychology provides the ideological legitimation for our relentless measuring activities.

Nowhere is this more evident than in the school systems where education and learning are thought of almost exclusively in performance terms. To ask what your child is learning has pretty much come to mean how well is your child performing. We have got to the point where we can hardly think of learning apart from performance because we lack the language to understand real learning. Schoolteachers today are encouraged to speak the language of psychology, which means they tend to view learning solely in terms of measured performance. And this is another reason that parents have become junior, or limited, rather than full partners in their child's education. For all their exposure to their own psychological experts in raising children, parents remain amateurs and "unprofessional" compared to teachers who have drunk heavily at the fountain of academic psychology. Thus, while parents are urged to be supportive and involved, they are expected to leave the "real teaching" of their children to professionals much better versed in the psychological sciences of growth, development and learning.

In the classroom it is the psychologist who can scientifically inform the teacher what to expect from students, how to measure it, what the measurement "means," and, more significantly, how to correct deviations from the norm. Many examples could be given about the profusion of measurement in the classroom, but I'll restrict my focus to standardized tests, the bane of so many children today.

What started so innocently at the turn of the century with Binet's attempts to devise a scale to measure age-specific intelligence in identifying retarded children has produced over time a

The Early Years

whole technology and industry of tests and scales, machine-graded and scored, standardized for group norms, that no worthy educational system can now live without. Standardized tests of basic skills have not only hurried children through schooling, but have created terrific pressure on pupils to perform early, often and well. Test anxiety has come of age now in the primary grade levels.

And the anxiety of measurement is not only felt by school-age children, but increasingly by teachers and principals who must convince school boards and other external groups that their students are indeed measuring up. Students' ability to score well on standardized tests is now the "measure" of good teaching and good administration as school districts compete with cross-town rivals to see which schools score highest. As Elkind contends, such emphasis only serves to strengthen the factory-like quality of our schools; we become obsessed with a measurable educational product and outcome. Moreover, teachers lose their sense of independent status as they become part of "management systems" geared toward goal setting, scheduling and monitoring class progress toward objective, measurable educational aims.

Social critic Kenneth Keniston points out that our educational system is no longer interested in the kind of human being promoted but in how well reading scores advance or decline.[19] And quantitative measures, so commonplace in the adult economic system, now are being used as the primary measurement of our children's worth. We have, in fact, taken much of the language and metaphors of our economic life to describe and think about education. Education has become a commodity, purchased at a price, the worth of which is measured in objective dollars-and-cents terms.

Thus schools and their participants, teachers, pupils and administrators alike, are under great pressure to perform well on each new batch of tests to measure some kind of performance valued in the larger culture. That some of the abilities tested are of intrinsic value and importance in a technological/industrial culture, there is no argument. But when the tests themselves, and the corresponding measurement scores, are pursued for their own sake, or serve to dehumanize learning and learners, or create undue pressures for children to perform, they can only do a disservice to real learning.

The present situation is causing many of our best and most dedicated teachers to question whether school teaching is a worthwhile profession anymore. Many are quitting the profession altogether. *U.S. News & World Report* recently examined the problems facing our schools and found widespread teacher dissatisfaction.[20] Judy Korn of St. Louis was one of them. A ten-year veteran of public school teaching, Ms. Korn began with high ideals and a desire to help children learn. Then followed the pressure and subsequent disillusionment that many teachers face. She found herself teaching for test scores rather than for real learning. In her last position as a teacher, the school principal complained because some of her students scored below the national average on standardized tests. While Ms. Korn felt that many of her students were doing the best they could, her principal was most interested in comparisons of their reading scores. Growing increasingly dissatisfied with what was passing for teaching, Ms. Korn changed careers and entered real estate sales. The message? If you are going to be judged in a competitive way, you may as well pursue an occupation that pays better for the effort.

Schoolchildren themselves are aware that emphasis on standardized tests often robs them of other learning opportunities. My youngest daughter, who graduated recently from the sixth grade in Arlington, Virginia, told me of the problem she and her classmates faced this year with the school talent show. This show had become an annual event and the students always looked forward to it. The show was not only fun but provided students

The Early Years

with an opportunity to work with others putting on skits, dances, chorus lines and so on. The principal of the school, however, decided to cancel this year's show because he felt students needed to concentrate their attention and energies on studying for the impending SRAs (Science Research Associates), a standardized test of learning comprehension administered schoolwide every two years. In his view the tests constituted a more important learning activity (that is, a measurable one) than the talent show, which he considered extracurricular.

The same mania for standardized test scores in reading and other skills also characterizes our obsession with measuring the "intelligence" of schoolchildren as a means of determining future learning potential. Happily, the worst excesses of intelligence testing are disappearing now, but for decades schoolchildren were tested for intelligence early in their primary grade career. Children who scored high were considered the brightest, more was expected from them and they were often assigned to accelerated classes. Students with low scores were placed into groups where the teaching pace was slower. Over the years, the "bright" students showed accomplishment (surprise!), received better grades, pleased their teachers and, with some exceptions, went on to high school or college. The slow students didn't do as well, and were gradually and subtly shunted into vocational and practical courses; many would eventually drop out of high school. We know today that the difference between what the brighter students accomplished compared to the slower students was due only in small part to differences in real ability. There is a "self-fulfilling" prophecy here. When teachers believe that a particular group of children is bright, they give them more attention and encouragement; they hold out high expectations and the children tend to live up to them. The converse of this holds true for students teachers feel are slow. The consequences are very real: the bright students tend to move on and upward, and the slow ones tend not

Measuring Up

to. What are the real differences in ability between the two groups? Probably not much. In our zeal to measure intelligence in some objective way, we have treated the "quotients" as if they were *real*, and have placed children into learning tracks that will, to a considerable degree, determine their future life in terms of high school diploma, college degree, professional white-collar careers, etc.

Often differences in early test scores reflect differences in the social background of the children rather than variations in natural ability. Working-class and lower-class children are usually at a disadvantage when required to show early ability on standardized tests. A school's tracking system is often a mirror of the community's social class and status divisions rather than the objective and scientific demarcations of students' natural ability. Appropriate here is my wife's story about her experience as a student in grade-school reading groups. Her teacher had divided her class into two reading groups on the basis of early tests of reading skills. Her group, the Bluebirds, was an accelerated group, while the Redbirds was the slower-paced group. As a child, my wife was not altogether clear on the distinctions between the two groups, so that when her mother asked her one day if her group had the best readers, she answered, "I'm not sure. But our group wears the nicest clothes."

Putting aside the issue of class distinctions, any child who wants to do well in our society had better measure up early; high scores are the name of the game in grade school. Today's children haven't the leisure for early mistakes and failures. They had better not be too slow to develop and find themselves; they have little margin for error.

Yet we know (or should know) that intelligence and other human traits and capacities are so varied, multi-faceted and complex that to treat them as a unitary variable with precise rankings is nearly ludicrous.[21] So why do we persist? Why do we

The Early Years

feel compelled to see our children as objects, and define their worth and value in terms of point scores, ratios and quotients? Maybe early testing of children makes good science and good pedagogy, but why should parents go along with it so willingly and uncritically? And isn't it time for us to accept our children as they are, the best and the worst in them, and love and care for them just the same? Why should we give up our children to educational bureaucracies buttressed by the psychological sciences and subject our children to those pressures? I am not blaming here any particular individuals for, as the saying goes, some of my best friends are teachers, psychologists and school officials. Most of them are very well-meaning, but they and we have permitted our cultural lust for measured, objective performance to determine much of the school curriculum and much of what constitutes teaching. More significantly, the performance ethic in schools has served as an all-too-convenient label of ability and potential, not so much defining what a child actually *can* do or *be*, but relying on what *tests* measure as ability or achievement. And on the basis of these scientific and objective tests we have consigned some children to the more rewarding and honored callings of our society, while others, who have come up short however early in their career, are eventually consigned to the lesser rewards of the lower rungs reserved for the "less able."

To what end is our preoccupation with testing children and pushing them to perform well in school directed? Can we have any assurance that what we are doing to our children in school is in any way promoting real learning or even enhancing a child's opportunities for success or creativity? I found it instructive to learn that many of Albert Einstein's teachers could not remember having him in class. When they did recall, they considered him dull; he was slow of speech. Thomas Edison was thought to be mentally ill by his teachers. In a study of four hundred eminent people in America and abroad, people like Winston Churchill,

Measuring Up

Eleanor Roosevelt and Albert Schweitzer, researchers Victor and Mildred Goertzel found that three out of five experienced serious school problems.[22] Many were considered slow learners, failing in subjects that didn't interest them, and disliking their teachers as much as their teachers disliked them. While many of the eminent were "gifted" and extraordinarily talented and creative, their talents and gifts were often at odds with school curriculums, and usually did not bring them praise, support and recognition from school authorities.

And what of the parents of eminent people? How did they measure up and perform as parents? Not very well, according to the Goertzels. In homes that produced eminence, parents were often "irritable, explosive, changeable, experimental."[23] And, I might add, so were the children who became eminent. They weren't often normal, as measured by some personality inventory. Creativity and contentment are not all that compatible. Only fifty-eight eminent personalities came from homes that we could consider "normal": untroubled, warm and supportive. The rest had to wrestle with a somewhat difficult family environment as well as cope with their lack of success and accomplishment in school.

Am I saying that parents shouldn't try to do well by their children, or that children shouldn't be sent to school? Of course not. As a parent and as a sociologist I know we must accept a certain amount of the culture as given. Nor can we all hope to raise children who will be the next Marie Curie or Margaret Sanger. These people come along rarely. But it doesn't mean we can't try to change things so that whatever Curie-like or Sanger-like qualities our children might have are not driven out of them in primary school by the pressures of standardized tests and grades.

And this is the point. Apparently few people rise to eminence because of perfect parenting or superior test scores and grades in

The Early Years

the public schools. Though people like Einstein and Edison would likely have scored very high on intelligence tests, the fact that neither these nor other standardized tests were administered to them in no way limited their ability to think, to learn and ultimately to change the world. The eminent will be productive however "deprived" of school testing and intensive parenting.

And I think the same can be said for most of our children, who are quite capable of leading creatively productive and authentic lives without being so carefully and relentlessly measured and tested (and thus screened) at every point in their young lives.

Parents too need to have confidence in their own natural abilities to parent, without feeling guilty or inadequate whenever their own inclinations don't square well with popular psychology, school authorities or the editors of *Parents Magazine*. We can learn something from the lives of eminent people when we see that the creative, the productive and the talented can originate in homes where parents were not perfect, not intensive in their parenting and not consumed with the desire to push their children to grow and develop. As parents we can relax, enjoy parenting, let our children be more free and less pressured and follow our own inclinations without fear that our children will end up as failures or disasters. And this kind of attitude is *not* the same as indifference or apathy. We can love and care for our children without being anxious about their performance abilities or potentials for future success. Parents can become people for whom children have nothing to prove.

I will return to this issue in later chapters when I offer a broader view of the kind of society that can release us from the pressures of the performance ethic and the excesses of the measuring-up process. First, though, we must continue our journey through the life cycle, examining how the performance ethic affects the lives of America's adolescents. As I've argued earlier, we must face the worst if we are to create a vision of something better.

Chapter 2

Why Teens Try Harder
Adolescent Life in America

The genius of *Peanuts*, one of America's most widely read cartoon strips, lies in its uncanny ability to capture adult humor and pathos through the trials and tribulations of children. Not too long ago, a *Peanuts* cartoon featured Charlie Brown and Lucy seated on a couch as Charlie thumbed attentively through a magazine and lamented to Lucy, "These catalogs with their models are depressing! Everyone is handsome and beautiful! Look at them in their new spring clothes. It sets an impossible standard for us kids. None of us can ever grow up to look that good." Whereupon Lucy smiles smugly and announces to him, "I will."

Leave it to Lucy and her irrepressible personality and gall to make a fool out of Charlie Brown once again. Yet many children, adolescents and young adults in America can surely feel and appreciate the significance of Charlie's fears. How can I grow up and meet the many standards the world has set before me? How

Adolescent Life

will I become happy yet feel that I have in some or most ways measured up?

Earlier, following the work of historian Philip Aries, we learned that childhood as a special, demarcated time of life was a fairly late development in Western societies, probably only a few centuries old. I think a similar line of argument can be advanced in thinking about adolescent life in modern society. While the idea of childhood took several centuries to emerge in Europe, adolescence as a special status between childhood and adulthood is likewise very modern, with expressions such as "peer group" and "teenager" being generally accepted within the past four decades.

My approach here is to view adolescent life in light of the performance ethic, as a stage of life infused with almost constant pressure on young people to measure up and to define their identities according to standards set by others. This measuring-up process which begins in early childhood continues unabated into adolescence as it magnifies and intensifies. Young women and men in our society gradually discover that much if not all of their social identity is fashioned from how well they have conformed to various performance standards that permeate adolescent life.

Assuredly, and I think most critics would admit, many adolescents today respond reasonably well to the variety of performance pressures. In a word, these young people have to cope with the demands by making identity and lifestyle adjustments. Indeed, to cope successfully becomes the hallmark of a well-adjusted teenager. And, similar to parenting, the contemporary adolescent can turn to myriad magazines, books and "how-to" manuals that sell advice, at affordable rates, on how to be a successful teenager. The messages are often slick and glib, always upbeat and optimistic, while the pages are glossy and colorful.

One does not need to be a professional critic, however, to

recognize that there is a dark side to American adolescence that is often ignored or minimized. We are increasingly aware now, despite our denials, that a significant and growing minority of young people do not cope very well in making satisfactory adjustments to performance pressures. A grim reminder of this fact was established recently by educators Charles Basch and Theresa Kersch, who in their study of adolescent stress pointed out, "Adolescents are the only age group for which mortality rates have increased in the recent past."[1] Moreover, this same age group now experiences disproportionate rates of suicide, anxiety, accidents and unwanted pregnancy.

Many would agree that the playful mirth of Lucy and Charlie Brown masks the uncomfortable reality that for a growing segment of our society's young people, the performance ethic is exacting a heavy toll. For a sizeable number of those adolescents who fail to measure up, drug abuse, psychological anxiety, suicide, eating disorders and running away have become all too common responses.

Peer Paralysis

During the past few decades much has been written and researched concerning the adolescent peer group and its extraordinary influence in the lives of young people. Most readers are now at least casually familiar with the findings of sociologists, psychologists and social workers revealing that few teenagers in modern society "go it alone." To be isolated, apart and alone is to become a virtual nonentity in the subculture of American adolescence. Perhaps the one condition most universally feared among adolescents is to be ignored by and isolated from an important peer group. At this stage of life the need to belong is highly stimulated, and this need for group acceptance drives individual teenagers to accept the performance dictates of the group. To

Adolescent Life

belong is to conform and live up to the standards of the group, whether the standards are grades, looks, affluence, popularity or whatever.

I'll argue here that maturation in the adolescent stage means, in part, that young persons no longer require or seek the supervision and guidance of significant others, such as parents and teachers. It is during adolescence that the "generalized other," the powerful, pervasive controlling effect of group life, becomes increasingly important. In a sense, the generalized other refers to society and culture. Yet the effects of society and culture on individual conformity are mediated normally by smaller groups, such as families, peer groups, organizations, etc. For modern adolescents participation in the peer group subculture is in reality learning to accept and live by the norms and values of the larger society. Of course, the peer group develops many norms, values and standards of evaluation of its own, some of which are in harmony with the larger society and others not. Little of this is terribly conscious or highly organized except in the instances of clubs or delinquent gangs.

Within the peer group each person is expected to internalize the standards of the group, judge for herself how well she is doing in measuring up to standards and apply corrections when necessary. On the surface, this all sounds like a growing maturity, what we might call "self judgment." The problem, however, is that very often the individual in the peer group does not question the appropriateness or suitability, to say nothing of the healthiness, of the group norms and standards. Many young people find themselves trying to measure up to group standards and expectations at the expense of their personal morality, physical health and psychological well-being.

Under these conditions we have peer paralysis: the inability, unwillingness and even fear of young persons to think and be on their own, apart from the group. When adolescents are paralyzed

Why Teens Try Harder

by the will of the peer group, they are not too likely to march to the tune of a different drummer, despite all the rhetoric in our society about human individualism. And, tragically, when some adolescents do attempt to break out on their own, they do so often in harmful and even self-destructive ways.

Peer paralysis is not possible, however, but for the fact that during adolescence young people learn not only to judge themselves but the act of judging others as well. The latter too is part of a growing maturity, to assess not only your own conformity to standards but to be willing and capable of assessing others. While adults become rather accustomed to their dual responsibilities as judge and judged, the nascent development of these capacities among teenagers can cause a good deal of anxiety.

Following this line of argument, my feeling is that adolescents "buy into" the performance ethic (many with a vengeance) despite the resulting anxieties that some of them experience. Teenagers and young adults soon find themselves inextricably mired in situations where they spend much of their time judging how well they are performing according to group standards and being the judge of their peers.

One possible reason for the fact that teenagers have adequate time to dabble in the higher realms of peer evaluation is that, increasingly, they have little else to do. In contrast to the childhood and pre-adolescent years, where so much of their time is filled with organized activities, teenagers are more on their own to develop the peer subcultures. And, while contemporary high schools are somewhat demanding on the time and energy of their teenage students, they lend ample occasions for peer group life to emerge and solidify. The more vocal critics of public education contend that many high schools do little more than "teen sit" for busy, working parents. While I would agree with this assessment in part, I don't think the modern high school and its administrators and teachers are entirely responsible. The issue becomes a

Adolescent Life

bit more complex when we take into account the pronounced changes in the American economy of the last few decades.

Given the shifts and dislocations of the industrial/technical economy in America, the fact is that there are far fewer employment opportunities for adolescents and young adults, at least the kind that pay well, provide upward career mobility and garner prestige. I'm not referring to counter and drive-in window jobs at McDonald's. In an effort to hold down unemployment rates and to parcel out the available better-paying jobs to adults, the entrance of thousands of young people into the labor force must be delayed. While few teachers and administrators would care to admit it, the American high school serves this function rather nicely.

Modern students find themselves enduring four years of high school in which the academic requirements, while somewhat rigorous, are rarely beyond the ability of the average student. Academic standards can hardly be made more difficult since high schools are under pressure to keep teenagers off the street and out of both the employment and unemployment lines. It is worth noting, of course, that in the suburban American high school, and within certain peer groups, obtaining superior grades is a source of considerable and intense measuring-up pressure. One cannot minimize the importance of grades among the upwardly mobile, middle-class and professional parents, and the pressures they exert on their children.

In general though, adolescent life and the high school setting provide sufficient time and opportunities for the formation of peer groups and their subsequent paralyzing effects on individualism. The peer group becomes the mediating arena for all sorts of measuring-up activities and provides countless opportunities for young persons to set standards and judge performances.

Importantly though, we must realize that the various perfor-

Why Teens Try Harder

mance standards of the peer group are not developed in a social vacuum. This could hardly be the case in America, where the relentless quest for capitalist profit often provides the impetus for social standards and expectations. The peer performance world itself is quite vulnerable to Madison Avenue influence. As many entrepreneurs of adolescent fads and fashion realize, there is money to be made in marketing products—music, styles and gadgetry, for example—to teenagers. A good deal of money. While Madison Avenue busily creates the need and the adolescent peer culture provides the group pressure, young people in our society live out their lives in a virtual counterculture of measurement in which their identities are assessed and defined by the cars they drive, the clothes they wear, the music they listen to. And this whole process is fueled by magazines catering exclusively to teenagers, providing myriad advertising images for them to look to in search of the measured self. In a heavily materialistic society such as our own, of all the ways adolescents can choose to judge themselves and others, nothing succeeds quite so well as commodities: things bought and sold in the teenage marketplace. Adolescents soon find the measured self within a commodified identity, where their sense of personal worth, value and even selfhood is evaluated not by who they are, but by what they can purchase, put on, listen to, or drive. It is within visible material fashions and lifestyles that the sense of self emerges and flourishes. But it remains a comfortable identity only insofar as the peer group continues to endorse the ultimate value of commodities.

The pressures on today's adolescent to measure up can often become contradictory. Especially for middle-class adolescents the requirements to perform well academically must be balanced with the pressure to participate successfully in the hedonistic subculture. By that I mean the activities surrounding popular music, parties, having fun, dating and "being seen" that teenagers are expected to enjoy and take part in. Though these activities are referred to as hedonistic, there is subconsciously a serious dimension to them. Young people cannot ignore having fun and being cool. There are standards of taste, style and conduct that are rigidly enforced and that teenagers must conform to. The individual teenager who desires to belong can neither ignore the standards nor easily hope to substitute his or her own.

Middle-class adolescents must keep one eye on their future college career in the hopes of getting into the right school, and the other eye on how well they are performing in the world of coolness, fun and fashion. Being able to achieve at a superior level academically may be possible only at the expense of complete and successful performance in activities after school and on weekends. How can one be admitted to the best universities after high school to launch a professional career, yet be popular, accepted, well-rounded and considered fun to be with while still in high school?

The domains I am about to elaborate are certainly not the only performance arenas; some readers will no doubt think of others. But I feel that the areas I have chosen are crucial and should give us some insight into the nature of the measured self in adolescence. The performance domains that follow are actually broadly based societal pressures that do not necessarily originate in the adolescent subculture but are mediated, shaped, enforced, and given unique meaning within the workings of the peer group. To some degree adolescents are living up to pervasive cultural mandates of American society. Yet, the forms of their striving, and its meaning for their lives, are to be understood within the specific context of the group processes that define adolescent life.

Looks: "Mirror, Mirror on the Wall"

A young woman from Holland, an exchange student at the university where I teach, recently commented to one of her

Why Teens Try Harder

professors concerning a puzzling aspect of American culture: "I can't believe that American girls spend a half hour putting on make-up to go jogging!" Puzzling perhaps to a visitor from Holland, but quite familiar and understandable to those of us familiar with the importance of "looks" in our culture. Those who would like to learn more about the subject among teenagers should read Jane Rinzler's *Teens Speak Out*.[2] Jane Rinzler, a teenager herself, conducted a survey of American teenage values and attitudes, and while her survey was not scientifically precise, her findings remain informative. She discovered that looks was the most important attraction among teenagers. And apparently the obsession with looking good dies hard even for those in late adolescence who populate our college campuses.

While the pressure on males to be physically attractive is real, it is the adolescent female who faces the most severe performance pressure to look good and make attractiveness a virtue. The adolescent female must develop a passion for her looks, a passion that is readily and continually stimulated by teenage magazines such as *Seventeen* and *Teen*. Even a cursory glance at these magazines is sufficient to understand the enormous concern generated by the advertisements about the importance of good looks. Virtually every page of a teenage magazine is filled with pictures of young women with perfect gleaming teeth, full-bodied stylish hair, unmarred complexion, ideally shaped face and figure; each of them is dressed in the latest fashion and styles. And the subtle message conveyed to the young female reader is that she too can look like that if she tries hard enough, or wants it badly enough, which of course she should. As might be expected, accompanying every picture of the perfect adolescent looks are the products — designer jeans, cosmetics, shampoos, rinses, acne medicines — products endorsed as being indispensable in helping the teenager create *the* image. What self-respecting adolescent female can

Adolescent Life

reject such imagery and the magic allure of the commodities, especially if admission to certain peer groups requires the kind of looks that at least approximate the ideal? Maybe she will never look exactly like the model in the picture, but at least she can try if she wants to be popular. And, if she wants to have dates. Rinzler found in her teenage survey that when it comes to dating, looks are the first attraction for males in choosing a date.

Thus adolescents learn two things about their lives from the latent messages conveyed by teenage magazines: first, you must have the looks if you are to be popular and dateable; second, commodities are necessary to acquire the looks. An acceptable self is purchasable; selfhood becomes a "thing," a market image. The pursuit of an identity has less to do with the recognition of inner qualities and more to do with an external commodified self that is thought to be within the grasp of those with the most money and best taste.

Complementing the obsession with looks is the adolescent's preoccupation with body imagery. Here again the strivings are most acute among teenage women who become as concerned with their figures as with their faces. The American cult of feminine thinness that drives so many adult women to health spas, dieting centers and diet magazines also permeates the adolescent world, where the obsession with thinness assumes cultlike qualities. There is ample research literature to document the unhealthy concern of high school females with their figures and I'll cite only one for the sake of brevity. Health researcher Robert Huenemann and his colleagues studied food attitudes and activities among teenagers in a longitudinal survey.[3] Of the teenagers in their sample, sixty-three to seventy percent of the high-school females were dissatisfied with their bodies and desired to lose weight. Moreover, the idea of "feeling fat" actually increased in the high school years, and twenty percent of the females in their sample were trying to diet. As we shall learn, the concern with

Why Teens Try Harder

slimness as a way of measuring up in the adolescent subculture often leads directly to eating disorders among women, with tragic psychological and physical consequences.

Physical appearance often forms the basis of status groups within the adolescent world which take on characteristics of subcultures. Such groups become virtually castelike in that once a young person is affixed to a looks status group, there is hardly any escaping or crossing to another group. The status groups, most recognized within the high school setting, take on names like "jocks," "nerds," "geeks," and are based on surface characteristics like body build, clothing style and physical attractiveness, as well as coolness in action.

Sociologically, we can witness here the power of the labeling process. For once a young person becomes labeled as a "nerd" or "geek" or "greaser," it becomes exceedingly difficult for him or her to overcome the often devastating effects of the label on personal identity and social interaction within the school setting. As an example, a young man labeled as a greaser might soon be cut off from the kind of social interactions necessary to do well academically or athletically, and might find himself forced to "live up" to the label. The resulting "self-fulfilling prophecy" may result in a series of bad grades, a truancy record and perhaps being dropped from school altogether. Using looks as a means of creating peer sub-groups can severely hamper the academic success of many young people whose looks fail to measure up. Virtually every teenager learns this upon entering high school and thus they become looks conscious themselves, knowing that to be otherwise jeopardizes admission into the favored status groups and risks academic performance. This very attitude, however, only serves to reinforce the reality and validity of the status group and further enables the labeling process to flourish. Adolescents create unwittingly the very structures and processes that they fear and which restrict their individualism and freedom.

Adolescent Life

Getting the Grades

While I argued earlier that today's high schools are not necessarily academically rigorous, middle-class youth cannot be satisfied merely to graduate and make average grades. Admission into prestigious and selective universities means having a superior academic record, and middle-class students must achieve high grades while taking the most challenging courses. These students can be in the uncomfortable position of having to do well academically, but not in a way that compromises their popularity. The teenage daughter of one of my colleagues was studying one evening last semester for an important exam in biology. This particular unit covered human reproduction. At one point the daughter interrupted her concentration and remarked to her mother, "It would be awful to fail... but, you know, it would be worse if I got everything right!" Such are the contradictions of academic life in high schools.

Receiving superior grades and garnering academic honors are important performance obligations for middle-class high school students for several reasons. In examining these we can get a better insight into the pressures on young people generated by the performance ethic.

To begin with, middle-class adolescents are under considerable pressure to please their parents, who want their children to do well academically as a demonstration that they are worthy of the thousands of dollars soon to be invested in their college educations. Also, parents are beginning to realize at this stage that they are rapidly losing the tight control over their children they have exercised for many years. Middle-class parents desire this last sacrifice to their dwindling authority.

Jane Rinzler's survey in *Teens Speak Out* informs us that what teenagers fought most about with their parents was grades. And

Why Teens Try Harder

the majority of parents couched the discussions of grades in terms of their importance for college and subsequent careers.

Rinzler's survey discovered much pressure to succeed among high school students. Fully seventy-five percent of the women and seventy-three percent of the teenage males said they had already chosen a career!

Grade pressure is also important among middle-class adolescents as part of general popularity and acceptance into certain peer groups. In suburban high schools, which contain predominately students from professional and middle-class backgrounds, superior grades and academic accomplishment are often the criteria for admission to the exclusive and prestigious peer groups. When this situation occurs, it is not surprising that parents encourage peer group life for the children as an influence to reinforce their own wishes.

In American society, for the middle and professional classes, success means graduating from a reputable university, and subsequently, graduating from business or professional school at the graduate level. While success might not be guaranteed by a college degree, in the minds of the American middle-class career success is hardly possible without it. The most selective of these colleges and universities set stiff academic barriers for admission—and aspiring high school students must measure up if they hope to be admitted.

Educational consultant Jan Krukowski's recent survey of American high school students found that students chose the "right" college according to what they perceive as the success of that college's graduates.[4] The more successful the graduates the more the students considered a particular college right for them, and the greater their willingness to get the kind of grades required for admission.

Thus many contemporary middle-class high school students create their own academic pressures because of their fears that

Adolescent Life

high school mediocrity (let alone failure) will deny them entrance to the kinds of universities they see as so instrumental to future success. A recent article in *Newsweek* on the "Privileges of Prepping" featured a survey of prep students at Taft School in Watertown, Connecticut.[5] This study found that seventy-five percent of the students indicated that their primary ambition was to raise their families in a comfortable lifestyle. Because of their family origins, these students realize the necessity of getting into the best universities in order to achieve this. Such attitudes raise concern among the teachers of these prep students who remember a time, now past, when attitudes were different. We hear from Lance Odden of Taft School: "When I first became headmaster, my task was to elevate their awareness of their academic responsibilities. Today it is to diminish their fear that some academic shortfall will translate into a direct interruption of their career aspirations."[6] David Elkind, a child psychologist who has written extensively about children and adolescence, puts academic achievement in the category of Type C stress situations: those that are foreseeable but not avoidable.[7] Elkind contends that for many adolescents academic achievement has now replaced the deep interaction with peers and adults in which traditionally young people learned their manners and conduct codes. Consequently, academic success becomes directly linked to self-esteem. Definitions of self-worth and personal value are tied to test scores and grades. Young people who do well in school are more confident of their self-worth and esteem; conversely, those whose academic achievements fall short of expectations see themselves in a less favorable light and develop a poor self-image. Elkind finds that when students begin to worry about tests, they can become angry at teachers for giving them and at parents for insisting that they study. Such students can develop cynical attitudes toward the school system. When academics become the basis for self-esteem every setback or shortcoming is a personal affront and takes something from each student's selfhood. Young people are sensitive to this situation yet powerless to change the process. Is it any wonder they develop resentment toward their schools, teachers, and parents? And this includes many adolescents who do well academically. Even the best students often experience an alienated relationship with their teachers because they realize the power of the grade to influence how others will think about them, and more importantly how they will regard themselves.

The Sporting Life

Traditionally the world of competitive athletics has been a male domain where young men were expected to prove their mettle and test their manhood in competition. Today, however, we have witnessed a virtual explosion of interest in women's athletics and in most high schools there is a significant number of young women seeing how well they can measure up on basketball courts and baseball diamonds.

Competitive sports and the American school system have worked hand in glove for many decades. We can hardly think of them separately. No doubt, athletics originally were viewed as a healthy outlet for students to work off the pent-up energy that resulted from sitting at desks for hours on end. Sports were considered a healthy diversion, especially for males who, it was thought, had the most energy to expend. High school athletic competition today is anything but an outlet and diversion as school corporations find themselves financing expensive athletic programs. Insurance coverage for football teams alone can become a healthy chunk of a school's budget.

Moreover, the success of many a school administrator rests on his or her ability to hire winning coaches; no principal can take pride in being the doormat of the athletic conference. Schools are often evaluated according to the success of their athletic programs and student athletes must perform well in competition for the sake of the school and the coach's job. Ironically, the athlete is expected to give her all for the honor of the same institution that during the school day administers all those exams she has come to resent!

The meaning of athletic competition in American society though goes deeper than the mere measure of a successful school district. Competition is at the very core of the American economic system, and successful athletic competition is linked strongly to the values of economic success. At every athletic awards banquet (college as well as high school) the student athletes are reminded that the lessons learned in sports are the same ones necessary for occupational success and career achievement in the American economy. Hard work, self-discipline, the will to win and teamwork are the hallowed values necessary for both a football victory and a healthy return on corporate assets. The captain of the basketball team is extolled as being only a few years removed from being a captain of finance. And just as the Battle of Waterloo was said to be won on the playing fields of Eton (not historically accurate), so are the successes of corporate mergers and leveraged buy-outs achieved on the football fields of American high schools.

The recent surge of interest in women's athletics in high school and college is tied to the increasing participation of women today in the corporate world. If the new women in American management are to be effective team players, they too must learn the lessons of teamwork in athletic competition, and there is no better place to begin than in high school or even in the lower grades.

While it is virtually heretical to criticize high school athletic competition in our society, one can be sensitive to the issue of whether too much pressure is placed on young athletes to be "winners," to risk life and limb for a successful program. We've

Why Teens Try Harder

learned recently the state of so-called amateur sports at many American universities, where players are paid, where academic standards are severely compromised in recruiting, and where any number of student athletes don't even graduate. Athletics at these Division I universities are more than preparation for big business — they are big business. Will we be able to say the same soon about high school sports, and the pressure there on student athletes to save the school budget, the principal's honor and alumni prestige?

While teamwork itself has many positive dimensions, can excessive concern with athletic teamwork at the high school level exacerbate the pressure of the peer group that adolescents already feel so strongly? Young people in high school, as we have seen, are preoccupied with the fear of letting down the peer group. Might athletic competition become simply another arena where the fear of failure can loom large and where losing represents something deeper than scoring fewer points than the opponent? In living up to the expectations of teammates, coaches, parents and school officials, just how free are today's young student athletes to fail, to lose and to admit that their play is only a game?

The SAT: The Future as Guesswork

The final domain of the performance ethic permeating adolescent life in America are the standardized exams now so commonplace in determining who will go to college and where. For middle-class youth this aspect of the performance ethic is especially keen; their chances of getting into the right colleges depend heavily on their scoring well on the SATs and the ACTs developed by the Educational Testing Service.

SAT exams have become a ritual in American high schools. They have taken on an existence as though they were decreed by divine authority. (Officials at ETS would, no doubt, like to as-

Adolescent Life

sume such a mantle.) Students, school administrators, parents and college admissions officers alike have accepted the SAT exams as a valid and fair method of determining who gets into which colleges. Students aspiring to be admitted to the "better" colleges and universities, however, come to view the taking of the SAT with a sense of dread, knowing that how well they score not only influences their collegiate futures but their sense of self-worth and their status in the peer groups to which they belong. For many middle-class students, taking the SAT has become a of rite of passage.

Those who have misgivings about the undue stress on SATs in high school are indebted to author David Owen for exposing the workings of the Educational Testing Service, which devises, administers and scores a host of standardized exams.[8] The ETS is a tax-exempt corporation that generated $130 million in revenues during 1983, paying its officers handsome salaries to work in plush offices and impressive surroundings. Officials at ETS like the idea that positions in our society should be determined by multiple-choice exam scores. They feel that superior and inferior ability can be scientifically measured.

Owen reasons that ETS is a powerful and yet unregulated monopoly determining the fates of thousands of people who have no option but to take their tests and live by the scores if they want to be admitted to a certain college, law school, or graduate program. ETS assumes a gate-keeping function, letting some in and keeping others out, depending on how they measure up on a series of multiple-choice questions administered on a certain morning.

David Owen's book levels devastating and deserved criticism of ETS and I shall not go into it at length here, other than to point out that test questions on the SAT are *not* necessarily developed by experts. Questions have only to be statistically reliable to be used. Nor are SAT scores a good predictor of college freshmen grades,

Why Teens Try Harder

having a success rate of about .52 at best. Actually, SAT scores correlate quite nicely with family income: the higher the family income the higher the SAT on the average. More important perhaps is Owen's contention that no official at ETS could tell him with any kind of exactness what "aptitude" really is. Yet, the test scores supposedly measure it precisely. We can only conclude that the SAT scores really form a mystique, and unfortunately for many young people a powerful one.

So powerful, in fact, that most high schools that want to do right by their middle-class students now offer SAT preparation courses. Students who feel pressured to score high on their SATs find themselves enrolling in these courses, spending time they could have given to reading, doing homework, taking part in a drama or musical. And the gist of these courses is to teach students how to take multiple-choice exams. They don't teach content or knowledge of a subject matter (let alone appreciation of it), but how to eliminate the incorrect choices given.

Of course, for families with money there are always expensively packaged programs available for private SAT tutoring. Many parents are quite willing to spend hundreds of dollars to see to it that their son or daughter measures up — after all, admission to the right college depends on it.

Over the past year or two, some of my students have been willing to share with me the pressures and anxieties they endured as high school seniors in getting admitted to the university where I teach. One of my students, Colby, originates from an affluent family living in a prosperous suburb of a large city, and he agreed to share parts of his diary with me. Colby appears a laid-back young man, his attire normally casual, loose-fitting but expensive preppie garb. During his senior year in high school his life was anything but casual and relaxed. Though he was a good high school student, Colby has the misfortune of having two older brothers whose high school grades were superior to his own.

Adolescent Life

College board scores were about the same — not too bad, but they lagged behind his older brothers'. Colby's mother was displeased with this and required an evening study table for him. He was to spend two hours nightly exclusively on SAT preparation. His two older brothers had SAT scores high enough that they found no difficulty being admitted to elite Eastern colleges. Colby had a lot to live up to, as his mother reminded him one morning some months later. Before he left to take his SAT exams, she said, "Remember how your brothers did, Colby. We expect the same from you. Don't let us down. You don't want to stay at home and go to a junior college, do you?"

It is my feeling that SATs and similar standardized exams are tyrannizing many young people, even those students who have done well in their school courses only to come up short on a set of multiple-choice questions. The case is, however, that educational leaders continue to equate high SAT scores with real ability and educational aptitude, despite the fact that the SAT has little predictive value. Daniel Regan, academic advisor for athletes at Villanova University, recently pointed this out when he argued that "SAT or ACT scores are the least reliable bits of information that one can gather about prospective students when they are compared with courses taken, grades achieved, and recommendations from high school teachers and counselors."[9]

As a university professor with over sixteen years' experience, I readily concur. The qualities I seek in a college student cannot be measured on an SAT and perhaps they are not measurable at all. What I look for is a love of learning and knowledge, a curiosity about the world and a willingness to risk something of themselves in order to learn. Through the years I have taught many students with high SAT scores who do well on exams, but who have little interest in the world of knowledge and ideas, whose curiosity is nearly non-existent and who take few, if any, risks. These students, and they are perhaps the majority, want a safe education, a secure future, a marketable major and a lucrative career. Such persons are all too comfortable in the measured self, and I wonder if this is now becoming the standard "product" of an education system that places so much emphasis on quantified measures of aptitude and even learning itself.

This may well be the case in an era of fiscal accountability that extends even to institutions of education. States are now finding legislatures willing to augment educational budgets only if the results are measurable. Thus, school systems will be pressured all the more to administer standard, quantified tests to students (sometimes even to teachers) to determine how much students have achieved academically, how capable they are for employment and how cost-effective the teachers and administrators have been. In a society that measures all success by the bottom line, there is a tendency to define education in the same terms, and seek only, or at least primarily, those results that can be measured and compared. In the scramble for scarce funds, losers will be determined.

But, is that what real learning is about? Will the corporate-quantified-accountability model provide the best education for young people? Are the only things worth knowing those that can fit standardized multiple-choice exams? And, more importantly, in an era that virtually cries for creative and resourceful solutions to problems, will the ability to score high on standardized exams provide the kind of leadership we need so desperately?

And what of the lives of adolescents, whose opportunities for learning, increased self-awareness and knowledge are sacrificed in favor of developing abilities to score well on exams administered once a year? How will they value real learning when they realize that much of their self-esteem and educational experience is represented by a single numerical score?

Adolescent Life

Troubled Teens

It remains now to describe the consequences of the performance ethic for adolescents. The measuring-up process claims many victims among young people. One can hardly read the morning paper or watch the evening television news without being exposed to a story of teens in trouble: runaways, drug abuse, eating disorders, suicide.

The House Select Committee on Children has released data showing that admissions to *inpatient* psychiatric services among children under eighteen years of age doubled between 1970 and 1980.[10] And more recent evidence gives cause for even greater concern: between 1980 and 1984 teenage admissions to private psychiatric hospitals increased 350 percent.[11] Persons knowledgeable in the field know that the problem of adolescent mental health is greater than these figures indicate because so many mental and emotional disorders go untreated, especially among youth whose families cannot afford psychiatric consultation and hospital services. These figures, disturbing as they are, might be painting only a very small part of an unattractive picture.

Not all youth are coping well with performance pressures, and many are frustrated in their attempts to find meaning and value in the measured self, though they might not be aware of the source of their frustration. And since the measured self is so common a pattern among young people, few of them are able to see alternatives for selfhood.

"Thin to Win"

As I pointed out earlier, adolescents are often overly concerned with body imagery. For males, the athletic, muscular build is a popular ideal; for females it is the thin figure. On the surface it appears that males are getting off easier than females, because the athletic build is usually obtainable through moderate weight-lifting, participation in sports, exercise, etc. There is mounting evidence, however, that some young men are resorting to the use of anabolic steroids, often illegally obtained, to build more rapidly the kind of body associated with male heroes.[12]

If some of the young men want bulk, most adolescent women desire thinness, and it is the relentless quest for thinness that all too often leads to eating disorders. We are becoming aware of the extent of anorexia and bulimia in America high schools and universities. The cultural ideal of feminine thinness promotes personal distortion and destructiveness. In this cultlike fascination with thinness, many young women are pushed over an emotional edge into the deep psychological disturbance associated with anorexia.

In an interesting study of cultural standards regarding feminine beauty, psychologist D.M. Garner and colleagues collected data from *Playboy* magazine.[13] They were particularly interested in the weight and measurement statistics of the centerfold models over the past twenty years. Not surprisingly their research documented a shift toward the thinner figure. They found the same trend toward thinness after examining measurement data in Miss America Pageants. However, and here's the rub, actuarial statistics reveal that the average female build for those under age thirty actually got heavier in the last twenty years.

Here then we have the kind of dilemma so commonplace in societies where cultural ideals and expectations are out of line with human reality and need. While magazine centerfolds are getting thinner, women are becoming heavier, creating a tension in young women that is accompanied by pressure to diet. As the ideal of thinness permeates the adolescent world is it any surprise that most high school females are dissatisfied with their figures and want to or already are dieting? How else can they measure

Adolescent Life

up? Feminist Susie Orbach contends that watching what you eat has become women's second nature as they try to adhere to the ideal of thinness.[14] Orbach also feels that most women don't question the ideal, they only feel bad when they fail to meet it.

Marlene Boskind-Lodahl has had much clinical experience with adolescent anorexia and bulimia, and she believes that, contrary to psychoanalytic theory, anorexic women have not rejected the feminine stereotype—they have embraced it all too strongly.[15] Their obsession with thinness causes them to accept the feminine ideal in a very exaggerated form. Baskind-Lodahl argues that anorexics want to please men as a validation of their self-worth. When they experience rejection (real or perceived), then self-worth is damaged and an eating disorder ensues. Adolescent anorexics are often high achievers and get good grades in school, not as a personal goal but primarily to please others or to attract a man.

From a feminist perspective Boskind-Lodahl feels that young women are socialized in our society to seek love from and eventual marriage with men. This is a woman's purpose in life. However, teenage women don't obtain the rewards they have been socialized to expect (love and marriage) because they are too young, and they are increasingly pressured to postpone serious courtship in favor of education. On a psychological level then, trying to please men is nearly an impossible task for adolescent females, and those young women who perceive it as rejection are often those whose sense of self-worth is seriously damaged. This spoiled self-concept results alternatively in excessive dieting and binge eating to create the "worthy" figure.

While certainly not all adolescent women become anorexic in the quest for thinness, too many do, and too many others, though not subject to eating disorders, are unhappy and frustrated trying to live up to an ideal that cannot be theirs or even bring them the satisfaction they hope for.

Why Teens Try Harder

Life and Death Matters

Adolescent suicide has entered the public consciousness with reports of copycat suicides and death pacts.[16] Much of this phenomenon can be linked to the deleterious pressures on young people to conform to impossible and contradictory standards. Yet there are tendencies to cover up and ignore what our culture is doing to young people, and to lay the problem at the doorsteps of the media. The argument goes like this: publicity about teenage suicide prompts other young people to take their lives as a means of gaining recognition and attention. This is an old and familiar line in America. We've used it to sweep away the importance and pervasiveness of public demonstrations and protests in the sixties, arguing that those young people wouldn't be protesting if television cameras weren't rolling and reporters weren't there to interview them. This type of thinking fits nicely with what sociologist Philip Slater calls the Toilet-Assumption about social problems in American society.[17] We don't want to face up to the problems created by certain of our cultural values, in the same way we want to flush away excrement that we don't want to live with. By putting our social problems out of sight we don't have to live with them; we can ignore their existence and refuse to deal with them, at least in any realistic and meaningful way.

Unfortunately (or maybe fortunately) this will not be the case with adolescent suicide and no amount of publicity can either cause or eliminate the problem. The fault is not in our coverage but in our culture, however reluctant we are to face that possibility.

Rates for adolescent suicide increased 300 percent from 1957 to 1975.[18] They peaked in 1977 with 13.3 deaths per 100,000 and leveled off at 12.5 per 100,000 in 1984. There are many studies of adolescent suicide from several points of view, and I shall not review them here. However, I think we can safely argue that

Adolescent Life

substantial numbers of young people attempt or succeed in taking their own lives because their sense of self-worth is severely tarnished or destroyed. Such young people feel that their lives are ruined and hopeless. They have tried to measure up to the cultural ideals accompanying their roles as students, males, females, friends, etc., and perceived rejection or failure. This combined with the loss of supportive social structures to be found in family, peers, church or neighborhood, generates the sense of loneliness and isolation leading to the formation of a death wish.

In his classic work *Suicide*, pioneer sociologist Emile Durkheim maintained that the breakdown of social norms and values associated with the emergence of industrial civilization cast people adrift morally. Many would experience acute anxiety due to the overwhelming number of choices to make without sufficient guidelines to make them.[19] One type of anomie (literally, "a-nomos," lack of meaningful order) is associated with the fact that most middle- and upper-middle-class people are socialized, particularly in adolescence, to believe that they can be anything they want to be, if only they "try hard enough."

Constantly forced to compare themselves with their peers athletically, socially, academically and in other ways, the vast majority of adolescents necessarily find themselves coming up short. Despite the cultural rhetoric that "the sky's the limit," most young peoples' actual accomplishments necessarily and inevitably run up against the real limits on their natural abilities, looks, etc. Moreover, even if they are especially able, the fact is that only one person can be captain of the football team, there are only a limited number of places on the cheerleading team and valedictorians come only one to a graduating class. Despite these facts, young people, regardless of their actual levels of accomplishment, are always measured against a norm of perfection, often reiterated by their parents. Faced with such pressures, relatively privileged young people can and do readily develop negative self-images which, in extreme cases, can lead to depression and even suicide.

Even working-class youth, who have failed to measure up to even the minimal standards of academic performance by dropping out of school, are transforming personal failure into group tragedy. Witness the shattering effects of a suicide pact in Bergenfield, New Jersey, where four "deeply troubled" youths took their own lives.[20] Three of the youths were school dropouts. Estranged in various ways from their families, they belonged to an outcast group known as the "burn outs." Rejected by the more popular peer groups, having failed in the eyes of school authorities, this tiny group gave up their lives together rather than endure the feelings of worthlessness and loss of self-esteem so vital to people of their age.

And how many lives will it take before we realize the devastating effects of the performance ethic and begin to recognize its pernicious influence among some of the most vulnerable of our people?

College Life and Late Adolescence

For some time now I've been impressed (not favorably) with the way in which the college experience has contributed to the measured self, and how the college setting permits performance pressures nearly as severe as the peer-culture of the middle teenage years. Since hundreds of thousands of young people in our society attend college, these performance pressures are worth looking at more closely.

What could the college experience be if we were to pursue the ideal of so-called higher education? "Higher learning" in America could be a respite from measurement and performance pressure; after all, one possible definition of university life is that of a community of scholars joining together to create, understand and share knowledge. Ideally the community would encourage a meeting of minds in which the younger scholars seek the wisdom and insight of the older, more experienced ones in a quiet, gentle, accepting environment where love for truth and knowledge is revered above all. Freedom to pursue the truth would be an essential priority. Moreover, students and professors alike would be drawn to the community because they share the same devotion to truth and knowledge.

Does this sound like the kind of university that most students in America attend? With some notable exceptions among the most prestigious and academically oriented colleges, I would have to say no. This is not to say, however, that within a good many universities there isn't a segment of teachers and students trying to create the kind of community I've described. The problem is that they are in the minority, and in their darker moments they know it. While non-university people often refer to college campuses as "ivory towers," that is not a very accurate description anymore. (Some academies would argue that it never was.) College life is rarely impervious to the demands of the world, even the tawdry ones, and instead of providing a respite from the measured performance that dominates contemporary life, the college experience at most places is largely an extension of it. The typical campus is rapidly becoming a setting in which few participants are safe from the measured self, as the identities of students and professors are shaped and given form by how well they measure up to a variety of standards, only a few of which have anything at all to do with love of knowledge and truth.

Most students find this out quickly. The message is learned even as high school seniors when they discover how intently interested college admissions officers are in their class rank, grade point average and SAT scores. They also become aware that to be admitted to the college of their choice it is these quantified measures that are most closely scrutinized by admissions officers and represent the bottom-line judgment. If students were privy to these sessions they would also learn that when college admissions officers really want to impress the faculty with the quality of the freshman class they have admitted, they often do so by citing their average SAT scores. A few thousand freshmen are categorized, evaluated by a pronouncement such as, "Their average verbal is 580 and that's up a few points." The faculty, particularly those in the English department, usually roar their approval.

For those in late adolescence and within the university setting, peer paralysis is not nearly so great. But there remains the performance pressures of grades, choosing the right Greek living unit, selecting a major that will please parents and being popular enough to get dates. In fact, it's my impression that the competitive, evaluative and achievement pressures are as severe in the university environment as anywhere in society; many, if not most, students see in their college experience an opportunity to prove themselves worthy and acceptable for the career they hope to launch upon graduation. I've had more than one student say to me that when they graduate they hope that the curriculum they selected and the experiences they had would make them "pretty marketable."

Human Capital

Parents of today's college students exert significant pressure on their children to perform well in school because in many cases they are footing the bills. Especially at expensive, private universities where tuition and room and board bills are extraordinarily high, parents shoulder an enormous financial burden. And they want something for their money. In many respects parents of students in private colleges have goals similar to legislatures at state-financed universities. They desire and even demand a good return on their capital investment. This is the meaning of the

Adolescent Life

human capital argument in education. Education is thought to be a worthwhile investment in a young person, providing, of course, the investment yields a good return. For many parents of students in private universities this means that their offspring will get good grades, choose a major that will assure a lucrative job at graduation, enroll in courses that look good on a resume. For some parents who really want to see their money work for them, they hope their offspring will join the best Greek living unit, and select the right kind of spouse.

I have talked to many students who realize the enormous price they must pay in performance pressure in order to have their parents pick up most of the tab for their college education. They are uncomfortably aware that they are no longer children but are an expensive investment, that for them to yield the kind of dividends their parents expect, they must indeed measure up in many ways. There is only the smallest margin for mediocrity or failure.

The human capital model in education was given much affirmation recently by former U.S. Secretary of Education William Bennett, a vocal critic of the quality of education in today's universities. Pondering the possibility of his ten-month-old son someday asking for $10,000 to invest in his own business rather than saving it for a Harvard University education, Secretary Bennett concluded that the business investment might be the superior one.[21]

With the human capital model receiving such highly placed endorsement and with many parents understandably concerned about the cost of a college education, what educational consultant Jan Krukowski found in her survey of American high school seniors is not a surprise.[22] Krukowski asked seniors how they selected a prestigious university to attend. When the students defined prestige, it had to do with their perception of the success of the college's graduates. Specifically, the seniors were interested in what percent of a university's graduates were admitted to law school, medical school and MBA programs, all of which represents preparation for well-paying careers. Even as seniors in high school the students surveyed knew their education had to pay for itself.

Getting Grades, Revisited

Based on my years of experience and the research literature in this area, my feeling is that the most significant identity peg for students while on campus is their grade point average. When all is said and done, and despite all the rhetoric about "learning for its own sake," the ultimate measure of a student's success while in college is the average of the grades received. Grades often determine students' choice of major, whether they can pledge a fraternity or sorority, membership in honor groups and organizations and admission into post-graduate education and qualification for fellowships. There is nothing quite as efficient and ostensibly fair as a grade point average requirement to keep some students out and others in when the university feels it needs to be selective about something. Nor is there anything as powerful as grade pressure to prod students into meeting a professor's expectations and demands.

The paradox here, of course, is that while the university pays lip service to the notion of learning for its own sake, the glories of knowledge and its pursuit, love of ideas, student success in college has little, if anything, to do with such lofty concepts. It makes little difference whether students adhere to them or not, as long as their grade point average is their entitlement to the privileges and rewards they have been socialized to seek. The embarrassing moments for college professors occur when students remind us of how hypocritical we are in this regard and just how nearly impossible it is to reconcile the ideal of "knowledge for its own sake" with the demands of a grade point system.

Adolescent Life

It has been my experience, though, that college students don't really mind the grading system that so completely envelopes their college experience. Since they have been socialized to see their college education as a capital investment, they realize the pay-offs must be calculated in measurable ways. Students want to be evaluated because their future success depends on it. My impression is that however pressured students feel about grades and grade point averages, they can't imagine any better way of staking claim to future rewards. Unfortunately, under current conditions, apparently the faculty can't either.

An extension of the significance of grade point averages for college students is the increasing importance being placed on Graduate Record Exams, Medical Colleges Admissions Tests and similar standardized exams college students must take to gain admission to graduate school.

Here again the Educational Testing Service fills its gatekeeping function as they help to select our future doctors, lawyers and professors. College seniors, who have already endured the four years of highly competitive grade-grubbing necessary to sustain a high average, now discover that their performance on a single standardized exam may determine the possibility of a professional career. Many students must experience a sort of "ETS deja vu," reliving the trepidations and fears of four years earlier when they took the SAT in order to get into the right college in the first place.

And, like four years earlier, they find they can get all kinds of help to prove themselves on GREs and LSATs and MCATs. At my university, where the lust for professional careers is especially acute, the hallway bulletin boards are covered with advertisements for Kaplan courses and the Graduate Admissions Preparation Service. For a healthy fee these organizations will help prepare students for the exams so crucial now in their lives. The Graduate Admissions Preparation Service is notably adept in its use of scare tactics to urge students to sign up. On one slick, colorful advertisement we read, "a single exam score may be more important than your hard-earned G.P.A." Or, what about this for pressure: "Competition is fierce at the nation's best business schools. Harvard, for example, only has room for about 600 out of the many thousands of high G.P.A. applicants. This may be your most important business decision: Are you willing to make a low-cost high-yield investment in your future?"

Even some professors get in the act by offering short courses in preparing for standardized graduate exams, and there are plenty of student takers. At most universities, mine included, this is serious business indeed as the university measures its own success by the number of its seniors accepted into law school, medical school and prestigious graduate business programs. When the numbers appear favorable they are circulated to the admissions office to lure prospective high school seniors. The whole process takes the form of a neat little cycle where universities try to measure up to each other by touting the success of their graduates and the selectivity of their admissions. All of this occurs at the expense of the students, both financial and emotional, whose successful grade point averages and acceptance records at professional schools are so necessary not only to their own careers and prestige but to the university's as well. Of course, none of this competitive cycle would be possible without the blessing and full cooperation of the teaching faculty — who are only too willing to bestow it.

Anorexia: The Problem Returns

I feel it is important to make one brief diversion into the special problems of female students. On university campuses the competitive pressure for grades is felt both by young women and men, especially as women seek careers in business, law and medicine.

In fact, for women to succeed in these fields they must often outperform men to gain recognition and opportunities. College women, then, are very grade conscious.

Aside from grades, though, college women still must measure up as females, and if the pressure to earn a "Mrs. degree" is pretty much a thing of the past (at least most of my women students say it is), there remains the pressure to be popular, dateable, have "good looks" and on some campuses conform to the standards of beauty and femininity set by sororities.

Given this situation, college women find the university milieu an extension of the high school environment, where looks count as much as brains and women are pressured to conform to feminine stereotypes of dress and beauty. The preoccupation with thinness carries over into the university setting, where we see women students jogging, enrolling in exercise spas, dieting and reading popular women's magazines for the latest figure ideals.

As we might expect under these conditions, eating disorders among college women have become a significant problem. According to student life authorities at the university where I teach, anorexia and bulimia among women are persistent problems. An interview in the campus newspaper with one of the counselors in the Student Affairs Center revealed that "... people at risk of having or developing a behavior problem with food are intelligent, upper-middle class achievers who want to be the best in all aspects of their lives." The same counselor went on to say, "I don't think it's being here (at this university) that causes women to have food abuse problems. A lot of people who I see have felt that kind of pressure to look and be a certain way for a long time, and they feel it elsewhere too." However, this counselor recognizes the unique pressures on college women with these concluding remarks, "The university is a very socially competitive place and it is representative of the media image of the way women are supposed to look."

Why Teens Try Harder

Through the views of an experienced university counselor we can see that women in college are often under the severe strain of having to measure up academically in ways that will assure them slots in professional schools or in corporate life upon graduation. But women must do this in a manner that affirms their femininity and physical attractiveness, proving that as women they have the right stuff, being able to do well yet look good. The often contradictory nature of these demands (for time devoted to looking good is often time lost to studying) takes its toll on too many women in the form of eating disorders, depression and other means of self-destruction.

The Resume Builder

Last semester in a course that I was teaching, our class discussion for the day centered on modern alienation and somehow the focus narrowed to the college campus and how students often join organizations in order to find social support. One young woman, Lydia, shed a different light on the subject when she told us she knew of several students at the university, especially seniors, who joined certain organizations in order to add things to their resume. When I expressed some surprise at this, Lydia took it in stride: "Well, you know what we students have become? We're resume builders. That's what counts now."

As is so often the case in these matters, students have a way of knowing themselves better than anyone gives them credit for. Isn't this precisely what we have been hearing about now for several years — the growing careerism among college students and the corresponding lack of social and political idealism? There is some truth to this, though I hope to show a bit later that the picture is a lot more complex.

But yes, students are resume builders because they are under tremendous pressure to make their education pay off. What better way to assess how well you have done in college than to be admitted to post-graduate professional school or to land a good job? The measured self among college students means proving to yourself, your parents and peers that you performed well and succeeded by signing your first contract. To that end most colleges today are committing substantial resources to their career centers. Students receive help in making career decisions, handling employer interviews and writing resumes and cover letters.

I'm always amused but somewhat chagrined to see senior males, who otherwise would never be attired in anything but cut-off jeans, T-shirts and dirty sneakers, show up for their employer interviews in three piece suits, polished dress shoes, dark socks, fresh haircuts and shaves. They are the picture of politeness and studied formality.

Of course, they know what counts most at that stage of their college experience. During the senior year the joys of extended adolescence in college are nearly over and the sobering reality of resumes, interviewing and finding a good job has just begun.

Looking good on paper can be just as important as personal appearance in landing a job; thus, students learn to load their resumes. If my student Lydia is correct, this means joining organizations you care little about to have a few more impressive items than the next person. Also, for some students this means avoiding certain situations and activities for fear of having them reflect negatively on a record. Students may not involve themselves in campus activism because an arrest might spoil their official record. More likely, student activism has little appeal to most students because it is hardly something employers look for on a resume. Political protest is not what is defined as campus leadership at the career center.

Resume building then emerges out of practical student concerns raised by career and placement centers and their officials. To get jobs, to measure up as a prospect, men and women must

Why Teens Try Harder

perform well in interviews, which means they must sell themselves. They must appear to be the kind of person an employer is looking for, even though they may not be. Campus interviews are exercises in impression management, not the presentation of an authentic and genuine personality, or of personal values, but the presentation of an acceptable self, a self that has been measured countless times and in a variety of ways has proven worthy of approval.

Resumes then are not much of what the student really is — only the person she or he can pretend to be. Even summer and part-time jobs are faked by being upgraded and retitled to make them sound more responsible and sophisticated than they really are. A clerk in a drug store becomes a member of the sales staff; a camp counselor is retitled a "recreation consultant."

Resumes can become dossiers in which students keep track of themselves. They provide their own surveillance now, and there is little need of student affairs offices playing Big Brother to the students, a situation so feared and despised by students in the sixties. Each student in the quest for a lucrative career or admission into professional school conducts her own oversight as she seeks an attractive placement file and impressive resume. In order to secure the kind of file employers seek, each student will police herself, avoiding the morally sticky situations and embracing those with good resume potential.

That students should become resume builders is not surprising, though I was startled to hear my student put it so baldly. Resume concern is rooted in students' fear that their education will not pay off, that the return on investment will be meager. Students are not very well informed about political and international events, but they know enough about the shape and direction of the American economy to be as pessimistic about it as many corporate leaders and economists. While there will be some

Adolescent Life

opportunities for young people, competition will be stiff and victory will go to those who measure up best.

The following headline is taken from the daily campus newspaper of a large state university: "Study says mergers are leaving many students unemployed."[23] This article describes for student readers the findings of a survey conducted by Michigan State University that mergers, acquisitions and downsizing are costing jobs in some of the nation's largest corporations. These companies anticipate significant cutbacks in the number of college graduates they expect to hire. Moreover, the higher salaries associated with the fewer jobs will go to applicants with the highest grades and best internships. And increasing numbers of college graduates will be tested for drug use and AIDS.

Not a scenario to inspire the hearts of college students. They now find that they must not only measure up in academics and internships but also be drug free and unexposed to the AIDS virus. What more will be expected of them as young adults? Is it surprising that instead of looking to build new civilizations or Great Societies today's students are concerned mostly with building resumes, placement files and a marketable self-image?

David L. Warren, President of Ohio Wesleyan University, spent the first several months of his new presidency living in the dormitories, getting to know the students there on a more personal level.[24] His impression was that the students indeed were frightened about their future, and thus they tended to insulate themselves through the acquisition of things and possessions. Maybe the truth here is that when young people can't be who they really want to be, their need to have is exaggerated; possessing things substitutes for an authentic life and identity. Readers familiar with the work of Karl Marx will recognize in that statement a very loose paraphrase of one of his central ideas.

Dr. Warren did discover, however, that deep inside college

Why Teens Try Harder

students was an element of idealism and concern for others, but it will not surface unless nurtured. And I might add here, not only nurtured but rewarded within the context of university life.

Are we indeed raising generations of young people whose only sense of accomplishment and self-worth is derived from those performances that can be measured, quantified and externally evaluated? Will our measurement mania drive young people so firmly into the measured self that there will be little opportunity for them to establish identities and personhoods that are in any way genuine? David Elkind has described American adolescents as *All Grown Up and No Place to Go*.[25] Well, in a society fueled by the performance ethic we might just as accurately identify them as "All Measured Up and No Room to Be." With so much of their lives measured and evaluated, and with so many of their activities geared toward successful performance, can young people find any meaning or value in their existence apart from living up to someone else's expectations?

I'm aware that some critics of my argument might remind us that these pressures are much worse in Japan; evidence is abundant that the Japanese are even more performance-oriented and competitive than we are. Doesn't the Japanese culture emphasize competitive extremes that even American capitalists worry about? We also have evidence about Japanese schools, that students there study longer, harder and in a more competitive environment than their American counterparts.[26] Aren't the pressures on Japanese youth even more severe since a poor examination score early in their school career can mark them for a low-level occupational career as an adult?

All of this may be true. It would be difficult to deny it, but I don't think we are led to conclude that our society should emulate Japan's just because their competition is more extreme than ours. I will have much more to say about this issue in the concluding

Adolescent Life

chapter of this book when we look more closely at the implications of competition for economic well-being and human life.

For now, though, and with respect to young people in America, I think it is hardly any kind of a balm for them to know that the Japanese student and teenager has it worse than they do. We certainly don't apply this rationale in society when it concerns our physical health and well-being. If it could be shown that the rate of lung cancer among the Japanese is twice as high as Americans, would we then consider lung cancer no longer a problem or reduce our efforts to find a cure for it? I hope that we wouldn't. Knowing that the suicide rate among Japanese youth is greater than among U.S. young people, which it is, should not make us rest any easier or deter us from seeking ways to reduce the competitive pressures our own adolescents are facing.[27] We must do this for the sake of our youth as human beings and our society's future since measurement mania has yet to establish itself as the best and only motivator of human effort and accomplishment.

I think we can conclude this chapter by arguing that as a society it would be greatly beneficial to define just what it is we want young people to accomplish, and what we hope or want for them as our future. Their voices should be heard too, as they speak about the kind of selves and identities they feel comfortable in. What if our conclusions drawn from dialogue center around ideas like maturity in leadership, generosity and caring as future parents, around sensitivity, wisdom and honest productivity as workers, neighbors and fellow citizens in a democratic, pluralistic society? Could it in any way be established that the best way to lead young people to these shared ideals is through constant measurement, unremitting testing and evaluation, competitive frenzy, quantified and scientific "achievement" norms and the encouragement of adherence to gender stereotypes? I don't think so.

Why Teens Try Harder

As we will see momentarily, adults in America are driven by the same competitive pressure and measurement mania we use on adolescents. Adulthood in the performance milieu is hardly any more humane, effective, or accomplished. New values and premises for human action must be promulgated if children, adolescents and adults are to be free from the constraints of the measured self.

Chapter 3

The Measured Self in the Middle Years

As in so many contemporary periodicals, *New York Magazine* runs a "Strictly Personal" column in which lonely, single, striving adults can reach out to other like-minded persons searching for the ideal lover or mate. Readers of the January 20, 1986, issue found the following classified advertisement among the many appearing that month.

> Inner virtue is what I'm looking for in a female partner — a strong identity, reinforced by solid ethical standards, consistently reflected in the way you lead your life. That is the kind of personal symmetry I respect and can grow to love. You should also be very bright (a graduate degree would be preferable), young (26–34), tall, 5'8" or taller, athletic (hopefully work out intensely several times a week and love one or two sports with a passion), healthy, physically affectionate, and very, very attractive in a natural, non-plastic sense. I am an over-educated, financially secure capitalist

The Measured Self

with his own successful investment company who is very tall, trim, muscular and works out every day. I love to ski, scuba dive, horseback ride, play racquetball, etc. I am told that I'm very attractive (used to model) in a natural way. Please send bio, photo (a must) and phone number. No smokers.[1]

Don't you wonder whether even in all of New York City there exists such a woman? And if she does, surely some man has gathered her up in marriage already. Or, one might be tempted to guess that any woman who can measure up successfully to all the criteria demanded by that secure capitalist would probably be a nervous chain-smoker or have already come completely unravelled emotionally.

And lest we imagine that such idolatrous concern with exalted femininity is an obsession that only swinging New York City males succumb to, the following is a personal advertisement for the unattached that appeared in the March/April 1986 issue of *Mother Earth News*.

> Dynamic, successful, strong, handsome, white Southern Christian, 38, 6'5", Ivy League, Europe education, real estate developer, animal lover, seeks innocent blue-eyed, Christian, country girl, 19–25 for permanent love affair, many children, country life. Ideally very bright, unpretentious, warm, soft, lovable, very feminine; likes animals, books, piano, older men, exploring life's mysteries; not drugs, discos, nightlife, fashion, feminism. Photo.[2]

Interesting, isn't it, that devotees of *Mother Earth News*, who supposedly have eschewed the trappings of modern technical culture, have themselves become victims of it.

Much can be made of these advertisements, but I don't want to run the risk of taking them overseriously. After all, it can be

The Middle Years

argued that although these men are seeking an "ideal," probably they will or already have settled for something less. Our Southern Christian might find a Jewish woman who otherwise fits his requirements; the secure capitalist might be satisfied with all he was looking for in a woman barely four feet tall.

However, there is something uncomfortable and insidious in these "personals" that seek perfection in a future mate or lover. For how many among us can measure up to standards such as these? And who would want to? Likewise, we might wonder about the kinds of men and women being created in our culture who would hold up such a measuring rod to a prospective mate. Whether these "personals" are intended to be mildly amusing or simply a puffing-up of expectations, they do point in a disconcerting way to the dehumanizing effects of the performance ethic in our culture. For these advertisements, as silly and unrealistic as they appear to be, show us how far the performance culture has come in reinforcing the measured self.

The adult years in America offer little refuge from the relentless pressures to measure and assess identity according to prevailing cultural standards of gender, attractiveness, success, etc. There is no haven today, or age of life, where such pressures disappear completely, though perhaps in the adult years they assume a special force, intensity and uncomfortable quality. The measured self in the adult years is accompanied often by a heightened sense of urgency, not felt in the same way by children and adolescents. For the younger a person is in our culture, the more life chances she sees before her. Failures to meet performance standards can be addressed and corrected by further schooling, self-improvement courses, orthodontia, popular literature, television and so on. And young people have relatively more freedom and time to develop an acceptable self and lifestyle. Their future yet lies before them, as they learned from various commencement speeches along the way.

The Measured Self

Adults in our society have a much more attenuated grace period; failures to measure up are not as easily forgotten or dismissed. While corrections for performance failure can be taken, there is an increased sense of immediacy. Failures in adult measurement standards can have not only quick and dramatic results, but there are far fewer years left to make adjustments and accommodations.

Career success, finding the ideal mate or lover and living up to gender expectations are all performance standards that tend to converge rapidly and forcefully in the middle years of life. Adults must successfully navigate these waters in the time span available to them. The future is now. The postponed dreams of youth — money, success, the perfect mate, the best of children — must now be realized. If not now, then when? Old age awaits, and in American society if you haven't "made it" by fifty, it's not likely you'll make it at all. Moreover, whatever your measurement failures were in your youth, the adult years offer a time of life to make up for them, to measure up and perform as you hoped you could all along. It is in the adult years that the performance culture offers the greatest, most unrestricted opportunities and rewards for those who succeed. But it is also in the adult years that failure to meet standards is least tolerated and most feared.

Reading the "personals" cited earlier, one cannot help but feel the sense of urgency in these males, that time is running out in their search for an ideal mate. Having proven themselves successful in business, they must now measure up in all things, in finding a culturally attractive mate to share their successful lifestyle. And perhaps what these two men dread most is not that they might have to live alone the remainder of their days, but that they have already "failed" to find the kind of feminine ideal so valued and extolled in American culture. Why must I resort to magazine advertisements, they must ask themselves, when other successful men I know have already found what they sought? In

The Middle Years

the adult years, the search for an ideal mate is now far beyond teenage fantasies, and the process of mate selection can become an anxious quest.

However desperate the search for an ideal mate might be, an even more central dilemma for adults in our society is the search for the ideal self. Indeed, our mates, those we think ideal, are really mirrors of our self-definitions, what we think we are and what we like about ourselves. But the quest for selfhood in a culture driven by the performance ethic is enacted within the measuring-up process. The self we can acquire lies within the possibilities offered by the culture, and as I've argued throughout this book, the possibilities of being are limited and constrained by external, consumer-oriented, measured criteria. As David Reisman pointed out some time ago, America is now characterized by the other-directed personality dynamic.[3] Americans acquire a definition of self neither in a commitment to an interior private ideal nor in the values and norms of tradition, but in conformity to the most current measures of a successful personality. Who we are is not derived from the well-spring of an inner life but in the response to what we think others are like, are doing, or what we feel others want us to become.

Parallel to the performance culture is the approval society. What we really want and seek ultimately is approval, to be well-liked and accepted. And what better way to accomplish this than striving to prove ourselves, to show that we can measure up in all things? And if our mates and lovers are both reflections and stimuli of our self-image, then they too must measure up and be worthy of approval. What our Southern Christian and secure capitalist are seeking is someone who not only validates their own lifestyle and values but someone who can draw approval from society.

The effects of the cultural performance ethic on self-identity are most pronounced among the middle and professional classes

The Measured Self

of America, and it is on their lifestyles, practices and pressures that I intend to focus in this chapter.

What are the measuring rods for successful middle-class striving? I would argue that they are many and diverse, but I want to collapse a large number of performance areas into three general domains of middle-class and professional life. Middle-class American adults are faced with measuring their life's worth and success with respect to: gender ideals (Masculinity/Femininity Dilemma), parenting (Supermom/Superdad), and the more traditional and familiar arena of social measurement (Status Achievement). The argument is that few middle-class adults are free from the performance demands in these domains, though on an individual level persons may make accommodations or attempt to carve out a life course emphasizing one domain over another. Not many adults in American culture can create an approved lifestyle ignoring the performance pressure in all three.

It will be instructive for us to examine now in more detail how the performance ethics in these three areas affect the lives of middle-class women and men, and the consequences for personal identity, family life and career.

Masculinity/Femininity Dilemma

In American society it is becoming increasingly difficult, if not impossible, for adults to lead authentically human lives because they are so pressured to measure up to gender stereotypes.

Historian Joe Dubbert has evidence to show that current male stereotypes date back to the original Puritan ethic which posited faith and work as the keys to salvation.[4] However, by the late nineteenth century work alone was the dominant goal of American males and the source of their identity. Of equal consequence, the developing ethos of capitalism held that long hours of hard work defined the "ideal man," and if he was too tired for home

The Middle Years

and family life, so be it. Capitalist values stressed that home and family were to become the province of women, where they could prove their femininity in ordering emotional life and domestic bliss. Moreover, males in the nineteenth century were expected to be intensely interested in athletic competition, because male character was thought to be forged in competitive struggles.

A similar line of argument is advanced by historian Peter Stearns in his analysis of gender socialization.[5] Both masculine and feminine imagery tended to solidify in the nineteenth century with the emergence of "middle-class" man, a rugged, competitive, sexually aggressive male. As might be expected, female stereotypes coalesced around the opposite ideal; women were considered sexually passive, emotional, gentle and noncompetitive. Males were assumed to be the more rational of the genders, therefore more suited for competitive careers outside the home. Women, too emotional to think very clearly, could muddle through work only in the home.

Industrial capitalism exploited the masculine image. Successful businesses were thought to be constructed out of the manly traits of competition and aggression, further strengthening the idea that business affairs were essentially a manly undertaking. Business was soon considered to be a battle; competitors were fought and economic wars won and lost.

Stearns contends that many men developed a love/hate relationship with business. While it was good that men were aggressive, it was considered a shame that they had to be. Eventually, there was a grudging recognition of the idea that men needed an emotional side. However, rather than giving room to their own emotional potential, males sought the needed emotional balance in relationships with women. The emotional female was necessary to complement the rational, aggressive male. Women were idealized as the morality principle, staying at home, displaying the essence of purity and goodness.

The Measured Self

The association of masculinity with work/business continued into the twentieth century, and even to the present decade, though accompanied by the male dilemmas of unemployment and loss of property. By the twentieth century industrial capitalism found it increasingly impossible to guarantee work for all men, and traditional male property rights gave way to large-scale class struggles for property and goods. How could the propertyless and unemployed males measure up to the ideals of masculinity? (This problem will be addressed more specifically with respect to lower-class males in the next chapter.) In very general terms, this is a dilemma for many middle-class males now. Unemployment threatens masculinity, and as sociologist Paul Goodman has argued, how can men "feel like men" when so much of the work they do is so unmanly?[6]

In the absence of job security, property rights and manly work, males must achieve prowess through consumerism, especially automobile purchases, which become a symbol of masculinity. The powerful, fast sports car allows men to exercise their maleness by driving aggressively and competitively. Males join in the automobile subculture, drawn to the enticing sexual imagery and themes of automobile advertisements.

Stearns contends that the "corporate man" emerged in the twentieth century—the male who measures up to masculine ideals of rationality, aggression and competition in his climb to the top of the corporate career ladder. Corporate Man risks failure, however, the possibility of moving down the ladder rather than up. Such a possibility represents more than an uneven career, it is an assault on the male's ability to live up to masculine ideals.

During recent decades a variety of writers have documented how the twentieth century has witnessed the solidification of this masculine ideal as the measuring stick for the American male. Lawyer and writer Marc Fasteau has described the modern male

The Middle Years

as a machine—not a real person but a stereotype.[7] Men have become dominated by the performance ethic because competitive performance is thought to be manly. Men can hardly think of themselves in other ways. The American male must prove constantly that he can measure up, but in doing so he becomes the stereotype.

Let's return briefly here to the personal ads. The secure capitalist and the Southern Christian were hardly persons at all. They were, in fact, stereotypes of masculine ideals searching for stereotypes of femininity. Describing themselves as strong, virile, aggressive, physically robust and secure did not reveal these men as anything other than someone desperately living up to the cultural ideal of masculinity. The proud bearing so unmistakable in these personals is not the assurance of someone who has achieved a degree of self-understanding and insight. While these two men profess a desire for women who are warm and passionate, there is little in their self-description to indicate they could reciprocate in any way. In fact, they seek qualities in a woman that are not only stereotypical for women but are the very qualities that atrophied in these men years earlier as they sought to achieve the masculine ideal. Indeed, they have busied themselves in what Marc Fasteau has called the "flight from passion." And having flown from the passionate ethic that could have been theirs, they seek it as an ideal, as a feminine stereotype, though neither man understands it, has experienced it, or desires it as a personal quality. Like men of the nineteenth century they want a warm, sensitive woman to complement their rational, aggressive personalities. Only in a relationship with a woman who represents the feminine ideal can these men feel completely human.

One gets the impression that these are macho-males, even though the decades of the sixties and seventies were thought to have softened the machismo element in American maleness, substituting a more pliant, gentle and sensitive masculine ideal.

The Measured Self

Whether macho-man as a male standard ever disappeared or temporarily abated for middle-class males, I think it could be argued that the eighties ushered in a period when the macho stereotype found renewed favor, support and recognition. Once again it was acceptable for men to act like real men and flex their muscles a little. Consider the box-office successes in the eighties — stars such as Sylvester Stallone, Tom Cruise and Clint Eastwood. Rambo dolls and other muscular fighting toy figures fill toy shelves in stores throughout the country. Clint Eastwood traded on his tough-guy image briefly to launch a successful political career in California.

Similarly the jingoistic political style of President Ronald Reagan and his often bellicose foreign policy have reinvigorated the macho in politics, where real men as heads-of-state won't be pushed around. Reagan's popularity in office, particularly among American men, was due in part to his way of reviving the sagging masculine ideal and his willingness to assume "tough" stances on issues.

If middle-class and professional men don't aspire necessarily to the Rambo or Dirty Harry ideal, they secretly admire their successes and approach. And while middle-class males might not have the physique of a Stallone, they seek the next best thing in physical fitness. Improving the male image currently means attention to bodily shape, and some ninety-two health and fitness magazines have been started since 1966.[8]

For modern males life can be thought of as a quest to measure up to the masculine ideals associated with competitive success, physical and sexual aggressiveness, rationality and coolness under fire. The problem for many middle-class males comes at mid-life within the area of occupational and career success. How well have I done? Psychologists Michael Farrell and Stanley Rosenberg portray the mid-life male this way: "He's likely to begin measuring his dreams of what he wanted to be against the reality of what

The Middle Years

he has become and the shrinking possibilities that lie before him."[9] As these two authors contend, most professionals peak during mid-life. If one has made it, fine; but if one has not, the stock-taking and self-appraisal are not comfortable and often lead to feelings of crisis.

Farrell and Rosenberg have documented that nearly one-third of the males in our society experience a decline in mid-life.[10] For many men the competitive struggle is difficult to maintain in the middle years, and the crisis that often ensues is precipitated by changes in lifestyle, values and societal expectations.

In her survey of American men in their forties, developmental psychologist Lois Tamir found that self-respect was a major concern for men at this stage of life.[11] And their feelings of self-respect are linked to their assessments of how well they measure up as men in what is expected of them. Living up to the masculine ideal and performing well contributes most to the feelings of self-respect and worth.

Current trends in the American economy will have direct bearing on the ability of many men to be positive about their career opportunities. As increasing numbers of women enter the contemporary job market and compete on more or less equal footing for scarce economic and career rewards, the opportunities for men to measure up and successfully fulfill the traditional masculine ideal will shrink. How many men at mid-life will face the reality of contracting expectations and possibilities as competition between genders becomes more intense? And what will it mean to the feelings of self-respect of men in their forties when they lose promotions and career opportunities to the women these men were socialized to believe couldn't be very competitive or aggressive?

One interesting way in which the competitive struggle between the sexes is being carried out is in the area of personal attractiveness. Steven Florio, who is the publisher of *Gentleman's*

Quarterly, acknowledged the new economic competition between men and women and how personal appearance can be used to acquire an edge. Florio comments, "Our men may want to look good for its own sake. But a large percentage of them are also competing with women for jobs, and they know looks count."[12] Thus, *Gentleman's Quarterly* readily offers its readers scores of advertisements for personal products to make men look good enough to measure up successfully against women. Here then is further extension of the commodified identity and measured self, a self that is not necessarily authentic or real but one lived out in appearances only.

For adult women in American society the performance ethic manifests itself in feminine stereotypes or ideals that women are supposed to pursue or measure themselves against. While the nineteenth century masculine ideal emphasized competition, rationality and aggression, the feminine stereotype required passivity, emotion and quietude. Women, especially those of the middle and upper classes, were considered too emotional and passive for the real world of work; their place was in the home peacefully tending to household chores and taking care of the children.

These images (and they do not always square well with reality) carry over into the twentieth century with some modifications. Although since World War II increasing numbers of women have entered the workforce, the feminine ideal remains — women fulfill gender expectations by success in mothering and being a good wife. As Nancy Chodorow (among other writers) points out, women's childcare responsibilities consign them primarily to the private or family orbit of life — the feminine sphere — while men's primary sphere is public.[13]

Probably the one change in the feminine ideal that took deep roots in the twentieth century was associated with feminine beauty. For the middle-class woman this means that the self is

The Middle Years

measured and valued with respect to attractiveness of face, hair and figure. As we saw earlier in the chapter on adolescents, women are socialized into the standards of feminine beauty as early as the pre-teenage years. Women are taught to be obsessively concerned with their looks, because their personal attractiveness is held up as the key to popularity, mate selection and later career advancement and economic success.

Looking into the mirror becomes second nature for women, who are taught from a young age that a girl never leaves the house without "putting on her face," that cosmetics are a girl's best friend and that next to a winning personality, nothing gets attention better than good looks. While boys are learning the competitive ethic, getting dirty on the football field, girls are being steeped in the beauty ethic at home, working on their posture, learning how to wear the right clothes and how to use make-up. Of course, I'm overgeneralizing here considerably, but my point is to show the early influence of beauty in defining femininity for young women. Women are socialized to see themselves as objects, symbols of sexual beauty, and to feel best about themselves when they look good enough to have others notice them.

Nowhere do we see the exaltation of feminine beauty more clearly in our culture than in the way feminine appearance is commercialized. Product after product is glamorized and made to look appealing by sexualizing it through the use of female models.

In one of the college courses I teach, my students and I view a remarkable film entitled *Killing Us Softly*, which portrays the devastating way Madison Avenue exploits women through advertising. We learn from the film that advertisers can make products sexually titillating and seductive by using women models in various postures and positions, embracing the product, caressing it. Another method product advertisers employ to demean women is in the use of glamorous, beautiful models to show off products

The Measured Self

intended to make a normal or average woman look as attractive as the model. Hair care products, cosmetics, nylon hose, undergarments and so on are modeled by women whose perfection in beauty, it is implied, is the result of using a particular product. As the narrator of *Killing Us Softly* reminds her audience, in real life even the models don't look that good. Pictures and films can be doctored to remove blemishes and slight imperfections in complexion or figure. Hours of preparation are necessary to make the model appear perfect.

Women's popular magazines, and there are many of them, could hardly publish a single issue without the cover page featuring a woman with a beautiful face, unblemished complexion, perfect white teeth and full-bodied hair. And the reader is encouraged — if she wants to look like the model — to find all the beauty tips, latest diet and current fashions necessary within that very magazine. If a visitor from another world had only magazine covers to go on in surmising what women looked like, he would never guess that some women have straight and gray hair, moles and freckles, semi-straight teeth and less than ideal figures.

Put succinctly, women's magazines portray the feminine ideal that few women can look like. The magazines, by and large, engage in a reality distortion that the average woman must treat as sane and sensible. While the fate of most adults is to become gradually bald, gray, overweight and a little dumpy, the ideals are held out to inspire us to be something we cannot. Few if any women can look like the models in *Vogue*, and trying to measure up to the impossible leaves many women with feelings of inferiority and even self-loathing, thereby damaging women's sense of identity, confidence and well-being. Women are no longer free to age, to dress as they wish, or to maintain figures that aren't sexy or alluring.

With more middle-class women today pursuing careers in business and professional fields, the cult of beauty is now com-

The Middle Years

bined with a "today's woman" ideal, emphasizing a feminine toughness, careerism and success. What many contemporary women's magazines hold up as the feminine standard is the complete woman, one who has great looks and figure combined with a successful career and manageable lifestyle. For today's woman, beauty or career success alone are not enough; both are now possible and worth striving for.

New Woman is a magazine billed for "the modern woman." Like so many of its genre, it carries the typical features of a contemporary women's magazine with sections on fashion and beauty, food and decorating, work and money and, of course, a physical fitness section. (How could a career woman dare be a few pounds overweight?) Sprinkled throughout its pages *New Woman* contains advice from doctors, psychologists, diet consultants and other experts, for how can a woman be expected to make her own decisions? The leitmotif of *New Woman* is that the successful woman today is a juggler and balancer who never lets her life stray too far in one direction. A woman should not pursue career success at the expense of her beauty, nor be so preoccupied with work that she fails to prepare nutritious meals at home, and she always finds time to stay fit and trim. The modern career woman must measure up in a good many ways, but with plenty of expert advice, product endorsements and recipe selections, there is no reason she can't perform well. Interestingly, the April 1987 issue of *New Woman* ran an ad for MENSA seeking new members. To join all you needed was an IQ in the ninety-eighth percentile. Let's see, have we covered all the bases for our modern woman: beauty, successful career, domestic excellence, smart money manager, slim figure, intellectual brilliance? That's not too much to ask, and if this woman is single, she will qualify for a date with the secure capitalist, providing she is near six feet tall.

The Measured Self

Fit-As-A-Fiddle

Among the recent pressures on women none is perhaps more severe than linking femininity with slimness and fitness. In this respect adolescent females are not alone in the pressures they face in keeping a slim figure — their youth just makes it a bit easier for them. Women in the middle years receive a similar message from husbands, physicians, magazines and actresses: real femininity lies in the ability and willingness to stay trim.

We might call this the Jane Fonda movement, where millions of women are trying to diet, exercise and jog their way into a Fonda-like figure and face. And Fonda's helpful books on exercise and diet sell by the carload and make her the ultimate winner. She jogs all the way to the bank. Recently, while I was browsing in a Waldenbooks store in an urban shopping mall, I decided to count the number of diet and exercise books. I found twenty-eight diet books and twenty-five exercise books; not a very scientific survey, but it gave me an idea of the popularity of diets and exercise, and just how far gone Americans are now. With health spas, aerobic dancing clinics, diet centers, "gut busters" and other instruments of torture, is there any good reason for the modern woman not to be trim, flat-tummied and in great health? Certainly no one can blame Jane Fonda for not doing her part.

As feminist writer Susie Orbach pointed out not too long ago, "right size" for women has been decreasing yearly since 1965.[14] And as we might expect, most dieters are women, most women are dieters.

Women are the target of a large commercial industry promoting books, exercise tapes and videos, work-out programs, running shoes, etc. Enormous profits are being made by entrepreneurs (Fonda is no exception) playing on women's guilt about their weight or their shape and urging them to conform to the feminine stereotype and measure up as "complete women." Slim and trim,

The Middle Years

bright, beautiful and driven are now the standards of the modern middle-class woman who turns to a commercial culture eager to sell her the commodified image that will win approval.

The February 1987 issue of *Ms. Magazine* sheds disturbing and important light on this phenomenon in releasing the results of a reader survey on addiction.[15] Chemical addiction appears to be directly linked to women's search for an ideal self. For example, sixty-four percent of the women surveyed agreed with the statement, "I would like myself better if I were thinner." Thirty-four percent who answered the survey experienced drinking problems, such as black-outs and memory lapses. And the drinkers tended to be women who experimented with a variety of dieting behaviors. Among the women surveyed by *Ms.*, self-esteem issues were critical in their lives and they intersected with food, appearance and relationships. Perhaps of greater importance, these women were concerned with their image most when their weight was up. In these periods they became excessively concerned with self.

Women are responding, of course, to part of the cultural performance ethic that places a great premium on attractiveness. They know what is expected of them. Women also know what happens to other women who fail to measure up. The research evidence is there. Psychologist Tom Cash, reviewing the experimental studies in this area, argues that we live in a culture where physically attractive people are perceived by others as being more poised, confident, bright and socially capable.[16] When these general perceptions are connected with the traditional and prevailing feminine stereotypes, the pressures on women for good looks are enormous. It may come as no surprise, then, that according to the *Ms. Magazine* survey, at any given time more than half the American female population is on a diet.

The Measured Self

Supermom/Superdad

Having examined the measuring-up pressures associated with gender performance in contemporary America, it is but a small step to the second domain of performance anxiety for adults. The terms Supermom and Superdad are becoming commonplace, and since much has been written about this issue our analysis will be limited to how the performance ethic has played a role in generating the problem.

The phenomenon of Supermom and Superdad translates essentially into "having it all," the attempt to measure up successfully to a variety of role demands, some of which are even contradictory. Having it all defies the traditional argument that division of labor was best for a healthy and happy life at work, in marriage and in the home. The traditional argument went like this: marriage, family and work roles were divided along gender lines, and men and women were socialized to accept their place in the division of labor and find satisfaction. Upon marriage the male assumed the role of breadwinner, working outside the home pursuing career success for the good of his family. To be a good father was to work hard and be a good provider. Women who married were expected to remain in the home, taking primary if not full responsibility for nurturing and socializing children, and keeping the home—cooking, cleaning, laundry, etc.

Scholars tell us that few families in America ever really fit this description. It is primarily a middle-class ideal that was reinforced through television shows in the fifties and sixties like "Father Knows Best" and "Leave It to Beaver." But we can understand the Supermom problem today only if we see the traditional gender divisions as a cultural ideal that was accepted as a way of life for several generations of middle-class adults. While some men helped their wives in the home and assisted with the children, and many women worked outside the home, the main

The Middle Years

source of role fulfillment was found in living up to the traditional expectations of masculinity and femininity. Whether men were successful around the home was only secondary in importance to their success as a breadwinners. And though women may have worked outside the home, contributing to the family income, it was the ability as a mother and homemaker that provided the yardstick of success. If troubles arose in the home, the wife quit work to restore domestic order.

Among the middle classes in America there is a blurring of role distinctions now, and a change in the way success in gender accomplishment is defined. More specifically, being a Supermom means that women seek success and accomplishment in all areas—home, marriage and career. No one role demand claims primary allegiance and success is expected in all. Superdad is faced with the same expectation and, to paraphrase the Enjoli advertisement and with a little switch in gender, Dad is to "bring home the bacon, fry it up for the kids, and never let his wife forget he is still a man."

The modern prototype of Supermom is Phylicia Ayers-Allen who plays Bill Cosby's wife on "The Cosby Show." Here is a woman who is a successful lawyer, a gracious, consoling and understanding mother to her children, and an intelligent, open, warm and supportive wife to her husband. And Cosby, for all his problems as physician, father and husband (without the problems of a comic foil there would be no situation comedy) is the perfect Superdad—urbane, witty, insightful, successful in the office, at home and in the bedroom.

There is much in our society that tells middle-class adults that they can have it all. Not only popular television shows, but "how-to" books, and magazines with advice and check points to instruct men and women on how to measure up, how to be all things to all people and do it well. But as most Supermoms and Superdads have found, the demands are often impossible, and failure looms just around the corner. *Ms. Magazine* a short time ago asked writer Pete Hamill to do an article about the new man who "wants it all."[17] Hamill travelled around the country to find out what it was that men wanted. The men he talked to had higher expectations for themselves than most women he interviewed. Men want a successful career, traditional marriage, wonderful children and modern independence. For example, here is the wish-list of a young stockbroker: supportive wife; a career for her if she wants one; must be great in bed; beautiful, with a sense of humor; and she has to be faithful. (Sounds vaguely like the secure capitalist again.)

The problem that Pete Hamill found for the modern Superdad is how to combine career and success, and have time for children at home. According to the *Wall Street Journal*, American executives work on the average fifty-six hours per week.[18] Not much time for home life.

Hamill concludes that "having it all" is an image of perfection being fed to young Americans who aren't very sure how they will manage. While it could turn out to be mostly fun like "The Cosby Show," for many young men the pressures might be far too great. When the chips are down, success for the modern middle-class male does not always or necessarily include changing diapers and chauffeuring kids to the day-care center. While home and family life are important to these career men, they can hardly aspire to be senior executives and still spend a lot of time with their children. Thus, for these men to be modern, their wives must be traditional, a blend that does not always work well in contemporary America. Witness the divorce rate of the past fifteen years, where nearly one out of two marriages ends in divorce (though the rate has slowed the last three years).

Supermoms have the more difficult ordeal says Carol Osborn, a former Supermom turned normal.[19] Osborn is the founder of "Superwoman's Anonymous," an organization providing support

The Middle Years

for recovering Supermoms. Carol Osborn had spent thirty-five years trying to be everything she could be: good mother, wife, boss, role-model. Ultimately she became very unhappy and felt miserable about herself.

She came to resent the Superwoman watchwords—coping, balancing and juggling. That is, all roles are capable of being filled to perfection with proper juggling and balancing of time and coping with problems. Osborn felt she was coming up short, experiencing failure and blaming herself for her inadequacies. She eventually discovered that she didn't even want everything.

As a recovering Supermom, Osborn now realizes how the popular media stimulate people's needs to have and be everything. Women are shown role models who can cope and be successful, but more often than not these are ideals few women can live up to. And if they could they would soon be exhausted, as Osborn herself found out when she tried to manage a successful business she owned, maintain her appeal as an attractive and stimulating wife and be the complete all-knowing, all-caring mother to her children. Eventually she felt physically and mentally drained, and who wouldn't?

In creating "Superwoman's Anonymous," Osborn discovered she was not alone. Pete Hamill also unearthed some failures in his investigation, as we hear from one of the Supermoms he interviewed. "'I tried,' a 42-year-old woman told me. An investment banker, she married at 35, had two children before she was 38. 'I tried like hell to put everything together and just couldn't manage it. Not because I'm weak, I think I'm a strong person. But there simply aren't enough hours in the day to be all the people I tried to be. The economy was booming, I was making good money. But so was my husband. I felt I was being a lousy mother. I was distracted at work. Something had to give. Sure I could have asked my husband to quit his job and stay home, but I don't think he would have done it. So I quit my job. I can't say I'm happier. I'm healthier. I'm less exhausted. I love the children. Of course, I also know that I tried to do something and failed. I'll have to live with that.'"[20]

How many women in our society, trying to be Supermoms, share the same kind of guilt expressed by this woman? Probably far too many, and is it in any way justified or necessary? Pete Hamill wishes things were different, and his remarks provide a fitting summary here. "I wish the relentless pressure in this country to be famous or powerful would ease up, so that more of us — men and women — could lead more civilized lives."[21] I would add to Hamill's list of societal pressures the need to be perfect or "super" in all roles. Only in today's Army can you "be all that you can be," and we should realize that, at best, that promise is merely an advertising slogan, and at worst a pressure few of us can endure.

Status Achievement

The third area of competitive pressure in American society, and perhaps the most traditionally recognized, is that of status and economic achievement. This domain is most directly linked to the myth of the American Dream, that through enough hard work, diligence and perseverance anyone can "make it" in America and everyone should try. And making it is defined in material and careerist terms — moving up the corporate/organizational ladder and becoming financially secure and prosperous. Americans are socialized to think of the pot at the end of the rainbow almost as if it were real and all the gold in it theirs if they work hard and want it badly enough. Status achievement is the most readily comprehended dimension of the performance ethic in American society because it is so directly measurable: income, number of promotions, size of home purchased, how many BMWs in the garage and country-club memberships. Unlike

The Middle Years

living up to gender stereotypes or Superdad ideals, which are often subjective and vague, status achievement produces tangible, material, countable and comparative results. In this area of performance the boundary markers of "having made it" are more known by oneself and others.

Author Gail Sheehy has documented fairly well how the middle years are especially crucial in the measuring-up process.[22] During this stage of life there is a good deal of self-assessment to see where one has been, how far up one has climbed and how distant the top may be. For those in the age group 37–45, Sheehy argues, there is an obsession with money and material success, pressure to overwork and the gnawing and uneasy suspicion that this may be the last opportunity to break away from the pack. Am I trapped and is it too late — the anxious murmurings of men (and more and more women) in mid-career who are uncertain about their future.

Historically, married women shared the status achievements of their husbands (they also shared in the failures) through the marital agreement; contemporarily, increasing numbers of women are trying to achieve high incomes and career success on their own. For women, fulfilling the American Dream has not been easy, because the corporate, financial and commercial worlds (in fact, nearly all well-paying work outside the home) have always been dominated by men. Women who want to make it must be all the more hard-working, talented, bright and persevering.

My wife recently attended a workshop on "Image and Communication Skills" sponsored by the Business Woman's Training Institute. The trainer that day was a young, energetic, articulate black woman whose motto was "Fake it 'til you make it." Her message to women who desired career success? Be very concerned about your image and communication skills. To be a powerful communicator one has to control the signals sent in nonverbal

The Measured Self

communication. She encouraged women to be aware of their style and image, because the style of communication is as important as the content. Thus, the open invitation to career-oriented women is to use images and signals to their best advantage as one way of making it in a male-dominated work world. Authenticity or genuineness in personality is far less important than the ability to create a powerful image through style.

Similar but even more detailed advice to career women is provided in Betty Harragan's best-seller, *Games Mother Never Taught You*.[23] Harragan makes no bones that career success is controlled by men, and women who want to measure up must beat men at their own game. Men who manage corporate structures organize them according to the rules they have been playing by for years. And since many men, especially older executives, have had military experience, and nearly all men have had a lifetime of athletic competition, corporate rules are modeled after military structures and ball games. Women need to learn about how the military operates—the importance of chain of command, rank, loyalty, etc. Likewise, women must think of themselves as team players, learning the rules of the game and mastering positions and strategies.

Harragan urges her career-oriented women to adopt completely the measured self. Career success for women has little to do with what they think of themselves or their inner feelings. Successful women are those who can influence and manipulate men into hiring them, paying them well and promoting them.

Thus college women are encouraged to join women's sports teams because it looks good to recruiters. Women should travel, not to enlighten themselves but to learn where the job markets are. And joining organizations is important, for it sends signals to recruiters and bosses that a woman has leadership potential. Above all, women should avoid the liberal arts curriculum because that is not where the money is. For Harragan, the bottom

The Middle Years

line for the career woman is always money, and if it isn't, the woman isn't playing the game correctly.

Well, despite such sage advice for career-oriented women, "making it" remains a difficult pressure to live up to. Even female graduates of business schools aren't doing all that well. Business researchers Jacqueline Landau and Lisa Amoss conducted a survey of 1,200 graduates of a medium-sized business school and found that of those out of school five years or less, sixty percent of the women and forty percent of the men earned under $30,000 per year.[24] Only fourteen percent of the men and five percent of the women surveyed earned over $50,000. Landau and Amoss discovered also in their study that women were trying to combine successful careers with home and family commitments. And this latter obligation put their jobs in jeopardy by the companies they worked for since it was often assumed that the women didn't take their careers as seriously as the men.

Probably for these reasons and others, women find it difficult to penetrate the top ranks of American management despite the increasing numbers of them seeking careers. According to Barbara Everitt Bryant, senior vice-president of Market Opinion Research Company in Detroit, women comprise fifty percent of entry-level management, twenty-five percent of middle management, but only a tiny percent of upper management.[25] For example, only 1,000 women compared to 49,000 men hold top management positions in major corporations. And only 367 women sit on the boards of the country's top 1,300 public companies, compared to 15,000 men.

While many women are entering the competitive fray of status achievement, the fact remains that there is only so much room at the top, and the competitive pressures are becoming all the more severe. And though males might know the rules of the game better than women, relatively few men will realize their dreams. They will be forced to shrink their expectations and settle for less. But the performance ethic is so deeply internalized by career-oriented men and women that for many there is no turning back or setting sights lower.

"The New Calvinists" is an expression being used to describe young adults pursuing career success in Chicago.[26] Business dean Richard Thain of the University of Chicago coined the phrase in referring to the enormous devotion to work now being shown by the upwardly mobile. "This profound devotion to work is a phenomenon of the last four or five years. It's not just among MBA graduates either, but all the way up to the higher executives. The work week has lengthened for all managerial employees."[27] Long, grueling hours are now the key to success since today's companies no longer reward loyalty and length of service as promotion considerations. "The idea of turning fifty and coasting is dead. There are no free rides," says John Alexander, a management consultant who advises corporations throughout the United States on performance analysis.[28]

Sixty- to seventy-hour work weeks are now becoming the standard in investment banking and managerial consulting. The New Calvinist has little time for sleep, let alone home, marriage and family commitments. Relationships are relegated to the back burner says Melinda, a bank vice-president. "Sometimes I ache for someone special to be close to. But, to be honest, I probably wouldn't have the time."[29]

The current intensification of the performance ethic is having an impact on career pursuits and professional commitments in America. Where once bright, service-oriented professionals were going where they were most needed, today material success is the prime motivator. As an example, law clerks to the Supreme Court are abandoning the service aspect of their profession to pursue fast-track careers in banking on Wall Street.[30] With the lure of material wealth looming larger, time-honored professions such as the law are losing their appeal. And law school deans ponder the profession's future as investment banks raid their graduates for the best and brightest.

While not all can aspire to the wealth of a Wall Street investment banker, the obligation remains for millions of other adults to find some measure of success in the economic world. The good life is measured precisely in the way adult men and women make something of themselves and surround themselves with the trappings of success. Economic and work life are becoming less valued as ends in themselves; the satisfaction of creating, building, serving and producing are less important than what is earned, amassed, and how quickly one is rising. The measured self in this regard means that occupational life is not evaluated by the strength of internal commitments and satisfactions but how one's achievements compare to others'. To what degree do my accomplishments pale when compared to others, and how are others diminished relative to mine?

Perhaps nowhere does this comparison phenomenon, so vital to the measured self, manifest itself as directly as in high school reunions. What better opportunity or occasion to assess how far I have climbed, to compare myself with others who started where I did?

Two psychologists, Doug Lamb and Glenn Reeder, interviewed people attending a high school reunion to discover the various fears and trepidations that accompany getting together with old classmates.[31] Lamb and Reeder found that young persons were more comparative in outlook, but such feelings lingered for those some twenty years out of high school. One young woman was very reluctant to attend the reunion at all. "I didn't know how I would measure up against everyone else's accomplishments.... I'm mad at myself for being so hesitant and self-conscious about who I am and where I am now."[32] And another young man expressed his feelings of comparative worth: "I hoped I would find out what others were doing so that I could compare my progress with others of my graduating class. I didn't expect so many people to be so successful or as accomplished as I am."[33]

Those attending the reunion who were twenty years out of high school weren't so concerned about measured progress, but realized they were being compared anyway. Their feelings were ambivalent, yet defensive. One woman shared her thoughts: "I am content with my life and want to show it to others... I'm tired of constantly admiring other people's lives!"[34] Yes, indeed, but in a society that so relentlessly promotes the measured self, a high school or college reunion is no place to be for those unwilling or unanxious to put their accomplishments on display.

But not all those in the middle years in our society need a class reunion to remind them of where they stand. Their lot is to constantly compare and appraise themselves in relation to others. Every man and woman trying to make it in the years they have remaining before they grow too old, or the hour too late, know how far they have come and how far they have yet to go. Time presses in on their lives. The demands of the performance ethic require one more pay raise, another notch or two up the corporate ladder, and maybe the building of one last dream home. For these are the only criteria that will satisfy the measured self. And though living up to gender ideals and trying to be a Supermom or Superdad is important, in the final analysis it is still money and career success that gives meaning to life in the middle years. And while many women today are feeling pressured to have successful careers, for now, it's primarily the middle-aged male whose sense of self is measured by how much he earns, and the size of the home to which he brings his bacon. It is these males in their often-desperate middle years of achievement to whom Linda, the wife of Willy Loman in Arthur Miller's *Death of a Salesman*, refers when she begs that "attention must be paid to such a person."

The Middle Years

Excursus on Sexuality

The performance ethic has permeated sexual relationships among many middle-class adults, adding yet another arena in which men and women feel constrained and obligated to prove themselves.

Ideally, sexual ecstacy lies in self-abandonment as an escape from the tensions produced in a highly competitive, performance-oriented life. However, in many respects sexuality has become just another competitive arena in which the performance ethic dominates. Instead of the intimacy of personal fulfillment in a unique relationship with another person, the measurement ethic in sexuality produces questions like: "Do I get enough?" "Was it good?" "Am I good as a sexual partner?" And, by not so far a stretch, "Am I good enough as a man or woman, hence as a human being?"

Sexuality today has taken on a new dimensionality of technique, achievement and mastery. Since Freud, it's been believed that repression of sexual desire is the basis of neurosis. The sexual revolution, which began in the 1960s with the impetus of the birth control pill, taught that greater emotional health would result from more and better sex. A central tenet of the counter-culture ethos was that sexual frustration was a prime cause of aggressive and antisocial behavior: "Make love, not war" was not only a slogan popular among those opposed to the Vietnam war, but also reflected a belief that sexual liberation would lead to a less "uptight," more loving world, and even to the end of war.

But as the increasing sense of meaninglessness and anxiety associated with the "Me Decade" of the 1970s and the selfishness and materialism of the "yuppies" of the eighties has shown, it hasn't happened. Denizens of singles bars and others, married and unmarried, who jumped into the waterbed of polymorphous, pluralistic sex have begun to report ennui, dissatisfaction and boredom. Quantity, variety and technique, no matter how exciting they might seem, don't bring the kinds of satisfactions they had promised. Quantity and variety don't lead to quality. Mastering the techniques of multiple orgasms, simultaneity and the other criteria countless manuals and self-help books set forth to measure how well we're doing in bed, doesn't lead to fulfillment.

Such information is good, and undoubtedly has helped many people achieve greater sexual fulfillment. On the other hand, the availability of information on sexual behavior has led to the establishment of norms of sexuality, standards of comparison. People readily measure themselves and many become dissatisfied.

Performance Anxiety

Joan Liebman-Smith, writing in *Ms. Magazine* on a study of adult sexuality, found that many married couples felt pressured into having sex as frequently as the national studies suggested was the norm.[35] A number of couples in her study felt bad when their own frequency of intercourse fell below national norms, as if in some way they were abnormal or inadequate.

Sex counselors and therapists speak of performance anxiety as a source of psychological problems in the area of sexuality. One of the major reasons many people seek sexual counseling is that they do not have a desire for frequent sex, and feel abnormal about it. In recent years, not "wanting it" often enough has become defined as deviant; lack of sexual desire is often associated with psychopathology.

In addition to sexual desire and frequency of intercourse as measures of healthy sexual performance, orgasm has become a sexual mandate. One of the outcomes of the sexual revolution and the subsequent outpouring of books and studies on sexuality in adults has been the "orgasmic imperative," the idea that men and

The Middle Years

women *must* experience orgasm, preferably more than once and simultaneously. Sex therapists report that women experience strong pressures to define their womanhood and femininity with respect to the type and frequency of their orgasm.

Books such as *Any Man Can* by sex experts William Hartman and Marilyn Fithian extol the manly virtues inherent in multiple orgasms.[36] With the proper technique and frame of mind all men are capable of more than one orgasm during intercourse. And every man who desires to measure up as a sexual partner should learn to do it.

Marc Fasteau has written cogently and convincingly about how male sexuality produces performance anxiety, because for males, measuring up in the bedroom is part of fulfilling masculine ideals.[37] A real man is ready at all times. "Since orgasm is thought to be the only real point of making love, physically competent performance, delivering the goods, easily becomes the sole basis for men's sexual self-esteem."[38] Fasteau argues that men fear a liberated woman because such a woman will desire to be sexually satisfied (have her own orgasm) and men fear they can't do it.

The performance ethic in sexuality means that feelings are secondary; what counts most is being able to achieve measurable goals such as multiple and simultaneous orgasm. As both men and women become preoccupied with sexual technique, impotency often results. The more people try to live up to sexual norms the less they are able to do so, the less enjoyable and pleasurable is sexuality, and the less room there is in sex for love, emotion and tenderness. For many adults in our society, whose lives are already an endless string of performance appraisals, sexual bliss and abandonment is no longer an alternative to performance pressure but an extension of it.

The Measured Self

Sexual Anomie: Expectations Run Wild

The main ideology underlying the sexual revolution, besides the Freudian notion that sexual repression leads to neurosis, is that Puritanical attitudes toward sex involved widespread hypocrisy, double standards and unhealthy frustration of natural functioning. At the same time, however, magazines such as *Playboy* made "girly" pictures respectable to the middle class by putting them in a glossy context intermingled with serious fiction, articles on public issues, etc. Typically, the modern male, single or married, was for virtually the first time able to have an excuse for looking at pictures of nude women: "There are many good articles" became the screen, so to speak, behind which sexually "sophisticated" males could avoid the shame and stigma that had previously been attached to sex-oriented magazines and French postcards.

Such magazines, however, also had the unfortunate effect of raising the sexual expectations of many males. The male looking at the photos of young women in *Playboy* and similar magazines, as well as reading the descriptions of often esoteric, extensive sexual delights in the "Playboy Advisor" columns inevitably compares his own sexual experience and the characteristics of his sexual partners with the very high standards of beauty, performance and variety set before him in naked glory and tantalizing words. With few exceptions the reader would find his own sex life and sexual partner or mate lacking to some, if not a great, degree. One response would be to try to find partners to match or come close to those in the magazines, and in fact many have done this. This means, however, that women are forced to try to conform to a very narrow range of body type, appearance and other measured characteristics, which leads to dieting mania, anorexia, constant concern over appearance and other negative consequences.

The Middle Years

Similarly, contemporary magazines catering to modern, liberated women, featuring centerfolds of macho-men like Burt Reynolds and male athletes, create measuring-up pressures in males to develop the kind of muscles, moustaches and body builds necessary to be an attractive male. Hence, any man who wants to be sexy, appealing and worth having had better spend plenty of time in the gym or health spa.

For married men and women the sexual norms and body builds featured in *Playboy* and *Playgirl* magazines, while presenting enjoyable bases for daydreams, also undermine their tendencies to be satisfied with mates. The performance ethic can create the kind of sexual ideal that few can live up to, though many may try. Marital discord and frustration often follow when both partners try to measure up to impossible sexual imagery and demands, and as couples confuse what is real and important in their marriages with what is fantasy and probably irrelevant.

And so we have come nearly full circle now, seeing how the performance pressures that began in childhood continue into the adult years. From cradle to computer camp, from Little League to Junior League, from boardroom to bedroom, we relentlessly pursue the measured self, seeking approval and measuring our lives against quantified standards, impossible ideals and current stereotypes. Our culture promises individuality and personal freedom, but delivers mostly a tight conformity and an identity gained through commodities and media images that can never really be ours. While on the surface we appear to be in control of our lives and destinies, we are actually driven by performance imperatives that demand us to be and to have what is faddish, unhealthy, impossible and often irrelevant to real human needs and desires. Thus we live the half-life partly for ourselves but mostly for others, and not always for the others who really count and care for us. We live for mysterious and generalized others hidden behind commercial images, media stereotypes and capitalist economic and educational requirements. Much of our interior life, our inner needs and desires, is sacrificed at the expense of meeting externally imposed standards that compel us without our knowing it. These are the perils, often unrecognized, of unconscious social forces that limit freedom and human uniqueness.

So far I've talked exclusively about how the performance ethic affects the lives and identities of the middle and professional classes of America. It remains now to assess the impact of the performance ethic on working class Americans, and the poor and minorities. For they too face measuring-up pressures, particularly economic ones, as they attempt to make a living, raise their families and have a life in a highly competitive, credential-oriented economic system. As we shall see, their economic fate and chance to live a humane life lie in their ability to measure up and compete for scarce resources in an era that demands more and more in the way of diplomas, degrees and credentials to make a living. What is the destiny of the poor and the working-class in an economic system that expects so much?

Chapter 4

Losers-Weepers
Dilemmas of the Underclass

One of the less expensive ways of identifying the values and beliefs of Americans today is to observe their automobile bumper stickers. While many Americans appear to have difficulty articulating what they stand for or believe in, their bumper stickers allow them to advertise a personal statement about something they think they cherish. A particular bumper sticker that made the rounds through various parts of America in recent years reads, "He Who Has The Most Toys When He Dies: Wins." It's been my experience that those bumper stickers show up most often on BMWs and Porsches.

Such stickers portray an interesting philosophy that blossomed in the 1980s, although it took root much earlier in our history. For America is indeed a society of winners and losers, of haves and have-nots, of overdogs and underdogs; and while in our past it was considered unkind and in bad taste for winners to flaunt their successes, the 1980s have provided unmitigated license for conspicuous consumption. In the competitive and performance struggle today, to the victors belong the toys as well as the spoils. And how are winners and losers determined in America? The performance culture plays a major role in determining who gets what, because in large measure winners are people who have "measured up" and succeeded: they have the best jobs, receive the best and most education and have performed well on myriad supposedly objective tests and appraisals.

Like most other industrial and technocratic societies, success in America has much to do with credentials — who can garner the most degrees and diplomas, the highest test scores and demonstrate the most "aptitude" on quantified scales. But it would be both inaccurate and naive to maintain that the fortunes of birth have no effect on this, because we know that social class, gender and ethnicity have much to do with who gets the best start in the credentials race. Here then is the obvious conflict between our ideals and our practice in America. While we purportedly value equality of opportunity, not everyone starts at the same place or with the same resources in the performance struggle. And though we would like to think that educational attainment, intelligence tests, scholastic aptitudes and other quantified and scientific measures of ability are objective means to sort out the "best and the brightest," the evidence now points to considerable bias in favor of the white, Anglo male.

Americans who want to think about it are faced then with an uncomfortable dilemma. On the one hand, it can be argued that at least in theory and ideal the emphasis on quantified, measurable and objective performance criteria has resulted in a successful economic system that, until a few decades ago, was second to none. On the other hand such an economic system, in creating a division between winners and losers, leaves many people far behind and deprived in a nation of plenty. And ironically perhaps, even the winners cannot be all that comfortable, for as we

Dilemmas of the Underclass

have seen in previous chapters, the measured self is never satisfied with material gain alone, no matter how important such an achievement might be in a materialistic society. Perfection in personal appearance, parenting for success and conformity to gender stereotypes are performance demands that make even "winners" uneasy and anxious about their lives.

However, this chapter is devoted to looking at those who are losing or have lost out in the performance struggle. Here we will examine the plight of millions of Americans who with each passing decade find themselves further behind in attempting to measure up. For the poor, the unemployed, for racial and ethnic minorities and women, their problem is not only the psychological assaults on feelings of self-worth that accompany poverty, joblessness and homelessness. Even more important are the material deprivations suffered by the many losers in American society who have no decent place to live, food to eat, or access to health care. Whether we want to admit it or not, the 1980s have not been good to those who lose. In 1983 for example, some 15.3 percent of Americans were classified as poor, the highest percentage since the 1960s.[1] Add to this figure the near poor, the unemployed, underemployed and those working for minimum wage and the ranks of the losers grow substantially.

Some will argue that a system of winners and losers will always result from a highly competitive and performance-oriented economy. Such an argument is not only plausible, there is an element of truth to it. It is difficult to deny that the performance ethic has served the American economy well through the years. One can say that the rigorous processes of measurement, necessary to insure competence among a substantial number of people, have been a major reason why our society has great importance as a creative force and is perhaps one of the most productive societies in the world.

However, two fundamental problems have emerged in Ameri-

125

can society that threaten the future productivity and success of the economy. First, the traditional and by now well-documented problem of equal access and reward must not be ignored. In an economic system that requires more and more credentials to "succeed," those groups that fall short on credentials will lag further behind in the performance struggle and are in danger of becoming a permanent underclass in America. Second, within the last two decades it has become increasingly obvious to many political and economic observers that American society is in a period of economic decline. Past dreams of unlimited economic growth, prosperity and international dominance are no longer being realized. Public attitudes reveal that many Americans are pessimistic about the future and no longer have a good deal of confidence that the economy will expand and deliver on the traditional American promises of prosperity for all who will work for it.

Indeed, both the processes and the effects of what some political economists call deindustrialization are well documented. The American economy, which was once thought to be unequaled in its ability to generate abundant industrial jobs and dominate international markets, now finds itself unable to generate nearly enough family-wage jobs or a competitive advantage over other industrialized nations.

These two fundamental issues intertwine to deliver potentially disastrous results. We must consider that there are millions of Americans who desperately need jobs that pay decent family wages, and offer psychic rewards. Yet many of these same Americans lack "performance criteria," the credentials and qualifications required for those jobs. Coupled with this is the general decline of the American economy and its inability to expand and generate the sorts of work opportunities necessary to lift millions out of the underclass. As the economy continues to produce fewer high-paying jobs, the credential crunch will become all the more

Dilemmas of the Underclass

severe in the scramble for the lucrative jobs that remain. Whereas a few years ago, a college degree was mandatory as entry for certain careers, today it is the M.B.A. or more. And if college students are feeling the pressure, what must be the sense of despair among millions of Americans who have barely finished high school and have no college prospects?

The effects of deindustrialization are not encouraging. In 1983, for example, some 900,000 workers lost their jobs in declining basic industries.[2] A substantial number of these unemployed workers spent months and years out of work and eventually dropped out of the labor force entirely. Those workers who were laid off due to foreign competition were unemployed for an average of nine months. When they found jobs, they earned wages a third lower than before their layoff.[3] Women suffer profoundly too, and experience significant declines in income when they withdraw from the labor force and lose a blue-collar job.

For those Americans unemployed, underemployed, or just entering the labor market, there is now the promise of an ever-expanding service economy. Whenever political and economic leaders boast publicly about the increase in the number of jobs for Americans, it is usually this segment of the economy they are referring to, though they rarely get that specific. They have good reason not to. Service-sector jobs, though increasingly plentiful, are not likely to pay well or be the prestigious jobs that adult men and women can feel they have measured up in. More often than not, service-sector jobs offer minimum wage or barely above, hardly the sort of work that will enable a person to support a family, get ahead in life, or experience a sense of achievement.

In recent decades these have been the jobs most readily available. Labor economists Susan Shank and Steven Haugen document this process rather convincingly in a recent *Labor Review* article. Noting that the civilian unemployment rate was down to

7.0 in 1986, they hasten to point out that nearly *all* the 1986 employment increase was in the service-producing sector. Moreover, in 1985–86 the number of workers on factory payrolls "trended downward" to 19.1 million by the second half of 1986.[4] "Trending downward" is an economist's way of saying that substantial numbers of men and women lost high-paying jobs.

The general decline of the industrial sector in America is not a by-product of the 1980s, though we hear more about it today. Basic trends in the American economy toward the service sector have been noticed for some time now. Between 1950 and 1976 the economy produced 1.5 times as many jobs with below-average wages as above-average wages. And during this period two out of every three jobs were in two basic industries: retail trade and service. These two industries alone accounted for some seventy percent of all new jobs created from 1973 to 1980. (And by the late 1970s the increase in the number of people working in eating and drinking places was greater than the total number of workers in the steel and auto industries.)[5]

Clearly, jobs and careers that are lucrative, prestigious and satisfying will remain in short supply relative to the number of persons seeking them in today's market. Competition will be all the more fierce. In such a situation, credentials and objective qualifications will take on added significance and importance with each passing decade. Each year the "acceptable" SAT scores for entrance to the better colleges will go up, elite professional and graduate schools will seek and find students with ever higher LSAT and MCAT scores, and prospective employers will scan American colleges and universities for those students with the highest grade point averages and the most impressive resumes. Today an average high school record is tantamount to failure, and a mid-range SAT score is cause for suspicion about the success potential of an entering college freshman.

The issue of returns on education can be raised here. Are

Dilemmas of the Underclass

educational credentials all that necessary for successful job performance, or are credentials primarily a screen to keep certain people out of the better jobs when there is so much competition for them? The latter can be safely argued. Diplomas and credentials are handy, objective means for employers to screen people. Who can argue with a credential? Yet in the last decade the median education level of those persons unemployed has been very close to the employed.[6] There is mounting evidence that increasing educational levels for jobs are often not linked to the performance requirements of those jobs. The cab driver with a Ph.D. is not necessarily a fiction.

Before examining more closely the flaws and pitfalls of a credentialed society, a word about equality of opportunity is necessary. First, if qualifications and credentials are necessary for one in our society to have any chance of career success, the question of equal access to opportunities must be raised. In the 1960s, America embarked on an ambitious plan to open up opportunity and mobility channels to millions of citizens who by virtue of their race, ethnicity or penury were left out. The general trend of social policy, at least on the national level, was to ensure that as many people as possible got a chance to measure up, to prove themselves. Reforms in access to education, aimed particularly at overcoming discrimination against blacks and minorities, were instituted. Programs such as Headstart were promulgated and welcomed by reformers during this era. In the economic and job sphere, the Office of Economic Opportunity, the Job Corps, and even the famous War on Poverty were thought to be advances in fighting unemployment.

But such programs had only limited success. Many open-enrollment programs failed, due in part to the inability of colleges and universities such as the City University of New York to instill basic skills in those students who had severely defective educational backgrounds. Affirmative Action programs led to widespread hostility among those whites and males who felt they had measured up, only to find themselves shunted aside in favor of minorities with lower test scores. The effort to compensate for past injustices and unfairness to minorities was perceived by many in the majority to be unjust and unfair to them.

Supporters of the equal opportunity programs of the 1960s and 1970s now argue that disadvantaged minorities did make some notable gains, and would continue to make more in the 1970s and 1980s had not such programs been under-funded and in some cases terminated. In other words, supporters argue, and in my estimation rightly so, that just as some progress in equal opportunity was being made, national policymakers shifted funding priorities to other areas (the Vietnam War and, later, huge defense outlays), and many of the social programs of the 1960s were allowed to wither away.

If by the late 1970s equality of opportunity as a national priority was a dying issue, by the 1980s it was firmly and unequivocally laid to rest as the Reagan Administration eagerly read the last rites. Today, with the exception of some activist organizations, Americans hardly pay even lip service to the ideals of equality of opportunity, the dream of providing greater access to minorities and the poor. In fact, we have witnessed in the 1980s the glorification of wealth and the virtues of private privilege. Television commercials now extol the "privileges of membership," the unbridled consumption habits of the Yuppies have been applauded and encouraged, and formerly idealistic college students now value economic security above human service. The Reagan Administration, with little fear of public censure, virtually ignored the plight of the losers in the performance struggle, as national policy focused most attention on the growing perils of international Communism and drug dealing.

As things stand today, a college degree is mandatory for career success, accompanied by high test scores, high grade point aver-

Dilemmas of the Underclass

ages and dynamite resume packages that no college recruiter can afford to overlook. Persons without college degrees, with the exception of those fortunate enough to find union-supported industrial jobs, are, for the most part, relegated to finding their economic futures in the low-paying, low prestige and high turnover jobs in the service sector. The college degree has become the "union card." Without it there is little need to apply.

This is the case despite the fact that work which calls for a college degree does not always utilize the talents, abilities and knowledge that the college-educated person has acquired. These are the dangers of over-qualification amply documented by economist Ivar Berg and economic historian Harry Braverman, among others. Braverman, for example, has demonstrated that many highly educated people cannot find jobs that require the level of education they have achieved.[7] Though they have measured up educationally, such persons find themselves in jobs that are not commensurate with their knowledge and skills. And Ivar Berg pointed out some time ago the tenuous connection between education and jobs in American society.[8] In a detailed study of job training, Berg found that over time the tendency is for substantial numbers of people to end up in jobs that utilize less education than they obtained. And in certain fields, such as insurance sales, persons with less education actually performed better at their work and earned more money. Berg also discovered that organizations and companies often hire people with high degrees of education but never promote them to the level where their education is needed. Such persons often quit because they realize that their superior education is not being fully utilized.

In a society where credentials count for so much in being hired in the first place, one is not advised to read the research by people like Ivar Berg. One is advised instead to get his degree and make the best of it, because a college degree remains the "measuring rod" of career potential in much of today's labor market. We have seen the power of credentials and measurable qualifications; we must now look at the plight of the uncredentialed and those who occupy the most disadvantaged positions in the performance struggle.

Women

The feminist movement has done much to raise awareness of the special plight of women in contemporary America. We have especially been made to recognize the economic hardships suffered not only by single women but women who have divorced or separated and now must raise their families on their own.

The women we might refer to as "traditional" are an interesting and often tragic case in point. Millions of women have been and continue to be socialized to define their femininity within the confines of marriage and family, urged to find their identity and fulfillment as good mothers and wives. These women lived by a traditional and historic but now largely defunct social compact that provided that their husbands would bring home a family wage. Being supported, these women would keep the home and be the primary nurturer of children. Such women sought, and many continue to seek, to measure up as good wives and mothers, gauging both their ability and their success within their role by the happiness and contentment of their husbands and children. More often than not, traditional women postponed their education beyond the high school minimum, as well as outside-the-home work, until later years, after the children had grown. Basking in their husband's educational and career attainments, traditional women traded their own attainments for the security of a lifelong commitment to a spouse who would always provide. After all, it was her performance as wife and mother that counted most, and many women never dreamed that the bubble could burst.

Dilemmas of the Underclass

As Barbara Ehrenreich has pointed out, these women never anticipated that the traditional social compact would erode rapidly because of the demise of the family wage system.[9] Equally important, movements such as modern growth psychology would tell men that what counted most in life was neither loyalty nor commitment, but how they felt and how they were growing as persons. More to the point, modern psychology was, in effect, telling men that if they were in a marriage that did not give them the freedom and space to grow and develop their fullest emotional and psychological potential, then it was time to change, to find a new partner in a more dynamic and challenging relationship. The male in mid-life crisis was portrayed in both academic and popular imagery as the victim of a stifling and stultifying marriage and home life. One of the cures was to leave.

This is an all-too-familiar scenario to traditional women, thousands of whom found themselves separated and divorced after years of marriage. Left alone to fend for themselves and their children, these women soon discovered that their postponed educations and work careers were their chief liability. What was once a loving sacrifice to their husband's ambition now hung heavily as they realized just how difficult it is to pursue an education in mid-life, or to secure a high-paying job without impeccable credentials. Very often it is these women who experience downward mobility; some of them will join the ranks of the new poor.

With their divorce, women become single parents while their former husbands simply become single. The economic implications are disturbing. Data from a University of Michigan Panel Study of Income Dynamics (conducted during the late 1960s and early 1970s) reveal that men who divorce enjoy a usable income rise of seventeen percent when adjusted for smaller household size.[10] Women, however, suffer an income drop of seven percent, adjusted for the shrinkage in their families. With some exceptions, divorce normally worsens a woman's economic situation.

Ruth Sidel has written one of the best books on women and poverty, and I will not attempt to duplicate her efforts here.[11] But I would like to rely on some of her research to bring home certain points. Sidel describes the "new poor" as those women who sink into poverty as they assume the status of single parent. Both factors are involved and it makes little difference which came first, singleness or parenthood.

Often the decline into poverty is dramatic and traumatic, especially for middle-class women who enjoyed a secure existence for many years. Sidel relates the experiences of a woman in her survey who, after twenty-three years of marriage, thirteen pregnancies and eight children, found herself confronted by her husband who "wanted out" in order to pursue his love for another woman.[12] She descended from a family income of $70,000 per year to $7,000. She faced the reality of living on occasional court-mandated child support payments (her husband left his job as well). As this source of income quickly dried up, she was forced to sell her household appliances to live, and shortly after lost her home to a bank foreclosure. Within a year and a half of her divorce this mother of eight children was poor.

While not all divorced, middle-class women will succumb to poverty as rapidly and dramatically as this, the fact remains that hers is not an isolated case. Indeed, she has company, and thousands of women in America can identify with her plight. Sidel points out that in our society, families maintained by women comprise sixteen percent of all families but account for some forty-eight percent of all poor families.[13] The impact on children, of course, is severe. Nearly forty percent of America's poor are children, and over half of these children live in a family headed by a woman. And if we look solely at adults, we find that two out of every three poor adults are women.

What about those women who pursue an education as an avenue to upward career mobility or as a hedge against divorce and the peril of single parenting? Here we find an interesting dilemma for women, one that calls into question the ideals surrounding credentials. In general, women do not enjoy the same returns on their education as men. Educated women continue to earn far less than educated men. In fact, many educated women have lower incomes than their male counterparts with less education. Data gathered in the 1980s reveal that for full-time workers, women with five or more years of college earn sixty-six percent of what males earn with the same number of years of college.[14] Even more discouraging for women who pursue college degrees is the fact that the median income for women with four years of college was $17,405, while men with only one to three years of high school earned a median income of $17,496.[15] So much for encouraging women to measure up in the college classroom as a means of getting ahead. While these women will earn more than females with less education, they will never narrow the income gap with males without major changes in the rules regarding sex discrimination in America.

This is not to say that women shouldn't acquire all the education they possibly can, because for the divorced woman with children, the chances of avoiding sustained poverty or near-poverty will be greater if she has a college degree and career experience. But even educated women will be less well off than men and thus less able to provide for the children than men, given the present structure of sex discrimination in earnings. Women with few educational credentials are much more likely to be pushed into the service sector of the economy, which we have seen pays less and offers few opportunities for upward career mobility.

Sociologist Lillian Rubin, in a remarkable and sensitive study of working-class families, describes the special plight of working-class women.[16] These women find that their aspirations for education and careers are met with stern censure, resistance and rebuke from their husbands, who want their women at home tending to the children. Here, the working wife is a threat to the husband's sense of manliness and control that he so desperately clings to as his identity and birthright. For the working-class male, a wife who wants to work outside the home signals his inadequacies as a man who can provide for his family. Working-class women are especially vulnerable to the economic vicissitudes of divorce and separation because often they possess few skills and qualifications for decent paying jobs to support children in a single parent status. While only some middle-class divorced women will descend into poverty, most working-class women find that divorce and poverty are nearly directly linked.

Blacks and Minorities

In a provocative series of articles for the *Atlantic Monthly*, writer Nicholas Lemann focused attention on the new urban ghettos of cities such as Chicago.[17] Unlike its counterparts of past decades, the Contemporary Ghetto is marked by despair and resignation. Formerly, urban ghettos were temporary stopping points for immigrant families seeking to move into more prosperous neighborhoods as their economic fortunes rose over time. Lemann argues that substantial numbers of black families, for example, during the decades of the forties, fifties and sixties were able to escape the ghetto as their economic situations allowed them to purchase homes in working-class neighborhoods and even middle-class suburbs. Much of this was made possible by the expanding American industrial economy of those decades.

Today's black and Hispanic urban ghettos, formed during the early stages of America's economic decline, offer residents little hope for residential and class mobility. The underclass described by Lemann is trapped, segregated and isolated in relatively permanent ghettos. Marked by high incidences of violence, teenage pregnancies, single mothers with children and predatory gangs, the modern ghetto offers its residents few visions of a better life. The contemporary ghetto is an island of poverty, virtually shut off from the rest of the city geographically, socially and psychologically.

While the female-headed family in general is characterized by high rates of poverty, race and ethnicity compound the problem and become the chief defining characteristics of modern ghetto life. Whereas the poverty rate for white female-headed families is twenty-seven percent, the poverty rate for black female-headed families is 51.7 percent and 53.4 percent for Hispanics. Poverty rates for children are even more disturbing. Of black children living in a female-headed family, sixty-six percent are in poverty; for Hispanic children the rate is 70.5 percent.[18] Experts now refer to both the femininization and minoritization of poverty. Being a single mother, either black or Hispanic, is almost a guarantee of poverty in contemporary America.

Ghetto poverty is not inexplicable, though the answers are complex. Unemployment and underemployment are surely critical factors. The Census Bureau documents that nearly forty-five percent of all black men do not have jobs.[19] Moreover, in 1980 the Census Bureau could not even locate between fifteen and twenty-nine percent of the black men aged twenty to forty.[20] It can only be assumed that these men have neither permanent addresses nor employment.

Unemployment levels among Hispanic and black adolescents is now well documented though little is done about it. In 1981 both sexes among Hispanics sixteen to nineteen years of age had an unemployment rate of 24.1 percent. Black teenage unemployment was even worse with 41.5 percent unemployed. Such figures are very high considering the drop-out rate of many urban high schools with large concentrations of minority students. Lemann noted some ghetto high schools in Chicago with drop-out rates of over fifty percent. Many well-meaning and dedicated teachers have virtually given up trying to teach their students in any serious fashion. Like the modern prison, inner-city high schools, populated mostly by students from the ghetto housing projects, are coming dangerously close to being little more than warehouses.

The effects of education on unemployment and poverty are not easily sorted out, but a few recent trends are revealing. In general, minorities receive less education than whites and enjoy less return on their education as well. That is, when minorities do attempt to acquire credentials and measure up, the pay-offs are not as great. This whole issue warrants a closer look.

Seventy percent of blacks finished high school in 1980, compared to only ten percent in 1940. However, whites still had much higher rates of graduation; in 1980 some eighty-three percent of white students finished.[21]

Minorities are persistently under-represented on American college campuses as well.[22] A report by the American Council on Education finds that minority access to higher education is lessening due to higher drop-out rates, reductions in financial aid and more rigid testing. Compounding the problem, state and federal funds for higher education are now decreasing, making it all the more difficult for minority students to attend college. Even more troubling is the Council's report that while the income levels of minority students has worsened, the focus of federal aid has actually changed to favor middle-class white students. The American Council on Education warns that if present conditions continue we could be heading for a system of educational and economic apartheid, in which highly educated upper- and middle-class whites preserve all the advantages for themselves.

Educator Stan Warren speaks of a "lost generation" of black college students, citing statistics that show the number of black students attending college may have declined by as much as twenty percent in the last decade.[23] And this decrease in the

Dilemmas of the Underclass

number of blacks enrolling in college occurs at a time when more black students than ever are finishing high school, with steady increases in ACT and SAT scores, and a rising percentage of students are taking academic courses.

Warren argues that the impact of the twenty percent decline in black college students will be felt in the decades to come and will be reflected in a decline in the number of black teachers, lawyers, physicians and scientists. The turn of the century could witness the most severe effects of this "lost generation" because as minority populations in America peak during this period, the demand for black professionals and educators will be greatest.

Can blacks expect their education to pay off for them in the same way whites do? Sociologist Reynolds Farley posed a similar question not long ago in a careful analysis of occupational and educational mobility among America's white and black populations.[24] Farley documented that, in general, blacks earn less than whites do, as might be expected. Though the earning gap is narrowing each decade, as recently as 1982 median income for blacks was still only seventy-one percent of median white income. Crossing gender lines, the gap widens as black women's income in 1982 was only fifty-six percent of white males.

More to the point, Farley demonstrates that investment in education pays less for America's blacks than for whites. For example, in 1960 the value of one additional year of education (in constant 1979 dollars) was worth thirty-five cents per hour for white males, but only twelve cents for black males. Two decades later a year of secondary or elementary schooling was worth forty-six cents to the white male, but only thirty-six cents to a black.

As we might expect, when looking across gender lines the differences remain large. Farley's data show that in 1980 an additional year at the precollege level was worth nearly twice as much for men as for women.

Losers-Weepers

We can see here the distinct possibility of an emerging and relatively permanent underclass in America, as two processes appear to have been set in motion. In general, returns on education are greater for whites (especially males) than for blacks and probably other minorities. And since the educational level of the unemployed is not significantly lower than for those employed, it is unlikely that substantial increases in education will have a profound effect on reducing black unemployment. What is likely to happen is that ghetto schools will probably continue to have high drop-out rates, though the overall rate of high school graduation among blacks is improving. And as Warren and others have indicated, minority enrollment is decreasing on college campuses, giving white students all the greater competitive advantage for those high-paying, prestigious jobs that require a college degree.

The traditional avenues to upward mobility in American society, education and an expanding industrial economy, are clearly not as accessible in the present decade as in the past. We are witnessing a gradual polarization in America of a privileged class composed mainly of middle- and upper-class whites who are well educated and highly credentialed, and an underclass composed mainly of blacks and minorities who acquire less education and whose educations are worth less relative to whites. The privileged white group will be able to feel they have measured up as they use their college credentials to pursue high-paying and honored careers. The minority underclass whose educational attainments will count for less will continue to occupy the lowest rungs of the occupational ladder, working at jobs that will rarely lift them out of inner-city housing projects.

The Credential Spiral

It is evident that we are reaching the point where credential inflation has replaced economic inflation as one of the most

Dilemmas of the Underclass

pressing problems. As sociologist Randall Collins pointed out in his study of education and stratification, education was the "weapon" traditionally used to obtain privilege in American society.[25] Credentials (degrees, diplomas, etc.) were a means of gaining access to desired goods. Today, however, the performance ethic in education has produced a high level of credential inflation, where amounts of education aren't worth as much as they once were. Too many people in America are now educated at high levels due to the massive expansion of the educational system; the impact of education on inequality is becoming negligible.

Blacks and ethnic minorities are becoming victims of a cruel hoax. For just as blacks increased their level of high school graduation rates to within striking distance of whites (in 1980, seventy percent for blacks and eighty-three percent for whites), high school diplomas don't count anymore as a requirement for high-paying jobs and honored careers.

Today the minimum for any sort of career (outside the unionized, industrial sector, which is not expanding rapidly enough to absorb large numbers of minorities), the kind of career a man or woman can feel good about requires at least one college degree. As noted earlier, for various reasons, not all of them clear, blacks are less likely today to pursue a college degree and graduate at the very time when such a credential is nearly mandatory. And the whites who increasingly populate the college campus, in an atmosphere where credential mania proliferates and intensifies, gain most of the advantages in competing for lucrative careers. If the credential spiral continues, the prospects do not look good for minorities in the decades ahead without either a major overhaul in funding for education (especially for higher education) or a reevaluation of how we look at qualifications for jobs and careers. Perhaps only the latter can assure greater equality and lead to a more humane way of allocating work in our society.

Credentialing in America is reaching the point where completing an education in and of itself no longer assures success. In some circles the thinking is that private, elite schools offer the best educational advantages for those who really desire to compete successfully for our society's most rewarding careers. And admission to the elite private colleges in America is often a matter of having proved oneself at private high school and elementary schools. If this isn't enough, for parents concerned that their children have a leg up on other children there are now the elite, private preschools that offer the very best in reading instruction, media centers and computer facilities.

Given this situation, even middle-class and relatively affluent families in America cannot be all that secure that their children can compete successfully for the best educational credentials communities have to offer. Whether they are correct or not, some middle-class parents feel that their children's journey to Yale or Princeton must begin in the best private schools, even elite and private preschools. "Preschool panic" describes mothers in an affluent section of Atlanta who were anxious about whether one of the handful of elite private preschools would admit their two-year-olds.[26] Trying to give their toddlers every advantage in a highly selective admissions process, some mothers offered to change religion if it meant getting their child admitted to a particular private school. Moreover, parents willingly subjected their two- and three-year-olds to psychological and intelligence tests as well as intensive interviews with admissions officials to select the brightest and most talented youngsters from the merely intelligent and average. Likewise parents considered yearly tuition charges of up to $4,656 a worthwhile investment in their preschoolers' educational future.

Obviously, even some affluent families in America do not feel secure in their ability to provide their children all the advantages. While affluent parents worry about whether their child has what it takes for a private, elite preschool, how can America's children

Dilemmas of the Underclass

born into poverty or into the lower class hope to succeed when private and elite educations are beyond them financially and otherwise? And how can public school systems, often overcrowded, understaffed and inadequately funded, offer the kind of educational experiences that some private schools do? The public versus private dichotomy in education now becomes another important screening device in America to determine which young people measure up in the competitive race for career success. Education in America is gradually discarding its democratic ethos (which may never have been too strong in the first place) in favor of a two-class system. For the affluent child there is the possibility, whether realized or not, of movement through a series of private institutions culminating with a set of impeccable and highly respected educational credentials to launch a career. For poor and working-class children, with some exceptions, there is the public school system tainted and even publicly maligned by educational leaders such as William Bennett saying they are inadequate to produce anything more than mediocrity. And while there may be elements of truth in Bennett's criticisms, how will the public school student's credential package compare with the elite when presented to employers?

It is not my intention to oversimplify and overgeneralize here, as we know that many students from the public school system "succeed" and some students from elite schools don't. And maybe that is the larger point. There is nothing inherent in this spiraling credential race that assures us that the most able, or the most hard-working or dedicated of our young people are going to succeed and achieve. Nor is there much in educational credentials themselves that guarantees our society that what has been taught or learned is even valuable in helping us deal with the critical issues of our time. There is precious little proof that these credentials really mean anything with respect to eventual success, ability or productivity. While in general children from affluent families appear to have advantages in attending private schools, their advantage is limited primarily to duplicating their parents' level of achievement, not necessarily surpassing it. And such children, despite their relative affluence, might not receive an education that permits them a higher level of self-knowledge, worldly insight, or productivity. By allowing a credentialing system to replicate the class structure, we are not using our vast educational system to accomplish its more important function of enabling all young people to achieve greater productivity, self-mastery and sensitivity to issues of human equality and cooperation. In short, education today has to be defined more broadly than as an experience to gain academic credentials necessary for careers.

There is some evidence that a century or more ago, our democratic ethos and a less complex economy combined to create a work environment in America such that minimum credentials in most fields were sufficient for a start in life. Success, productivity, reliability, resourcefulness and other work traits were tested on the job. After all, the so-called self-made men and women in America were often cultural heroes, those held up as role models for a younger generation. Obviously there was rampant race, gender and ethnic discrimination, but education in its present form has failed to eliminate such discrimination and has added the more subtle discrimination of credentials. At least in ideology, and to some degree in practice, in past generations people were able to rise and fall on their own abilities, aside from any educational attainments they might have acquired.

Today our obsession with academic credentials, test scores, grades, etc., assures us little beyond replication of the class structure, and giving corporate recruiters and graduate schools a sense that they are selecting the best people. Actually, there is little way of knowing whether they are or not.

I'm reminded of a television commercial of a few years ago that portrayed a young Abraham Lincoln in a modern employ-

Dilemmas of the Underclass

ment office seeking a job. The employment official began to question Lincoln about his educational background. Lincoln soon found himself hard-pressed to present any qualifications for a job the agency might offer. Shaking his head sadly, the employment officer lamented that while he would like to help him, there was little that Lincoln qualified for. His resume was so incomplete. The commercial message was on behalf of a metropolitan area school that offered the right kind of degrees and educational preparation for career success in today's world.

Now whether or not Lincoln would be a success in modern culture is beside the point. Fortunately, he lived in an era where ability, productivity and competence were not so neatly packaged. Lincoln could prove himself as a leader without the aid of intelligence tests, curriculum specialists and educational bureaucrats. Lincoln's superior abilities and talents were allowed to evolve and flourish in the practical routines of everyday life. Lincoln and others of his age were permitted the luxury that too few people experience today (especially young people) — to search for and discover their abilities in meeting the demands of the day, not in measuring up in quantified ways to educational standards and programs often remote from practical and worldly concerns.

If educational credentials were a truly adequate means of preparing people to be resourceful, creative and productive in the world, and not mostly a mechanism for allocating privilege, why does there appear to be such a crisis in leadership and productivity in our society? If the best and most able are supposed to reach the top in this kind of system, why don't they? Witness in recent years the public dismay with leadership in government, economy and even religion. What is the record in America? Gradual decline in economic productivity and quality of work while industrial leaders pursue short-term maximization of profits. Few economic leaders appear to have workable, humane and efficient solutions to re-industrialize our society, to say nothing of financial leaders on Wall Street, many of whom are committed to the most short-sighted greed, and even dishonest trading and secrecy. Our political leaders lack the courage to be more concerned with substance than image. Most of them are led in whatever direction public opinion polls point to. Moreover, this past decade has brought us nearly unprecedented levels of political chicanery, fraud and corruption. Watergate apparently was only the beginning, not the culmination, of modern high-level government corruption. And we have found little to give us confidence in certain religious leaders, who themselves have engaged in the most blatant immorality and deceit. This is all part of the record of top leadership in America, though I'm aware there are numerous exceptions and there are many able, talented and productive people in government service, industry and religious organizations. But surely we can do better in providing opportunities for more people to utilize their productive capacity, creativity and resourcefulness. Presently we permit credentials and "measured" educational achievements to substitute for more effective and fair means to insure that the most capable people have a chance to become leaders and to serve.

Are we not consigning a significant and growing portion of our population to poverty and neglect without even furnishing them real opportunities to develop their talents? Are not our actions nearly self-destructive when we continue to use supposedly objective and predictive educational tests and measures to screen out people whose abilities and potentials do not test well, or who are not "early advantaged?" One wonders how much needed talent, integrity and resourcefulness slips through the cracks of an educational system devoted to testing, curriculum paths, degree programs and measurable results. How much talent among the poor, blacks and minorities, who do not always test well, are we losing and neglecting at a time when the complexity of national and world issues requires the very best efforts of everyone?

Dilemmas of the Underclass

Empathy Failure

Several years ago, psychologist William Ryan, in a provocative book called *Blaming the Victim,* argued that Americans often blame the victims of social problems for their troubles.[27] Rather than search for fundamental causes of social problems it is easier for us to give the responsibility to victims for personal, psychological and subcultural inadequacies.

We see examples of victim-blaming most readily in attitudes toward the poor and minorities. Why are they poor and why do they suffer? Because they don't work hard enough, they drop out of school, or they lack the psychological need to achieve. The list of personal inadequacies cited is actually much longer than this. And once we have blamed the victim, we aren't required to look any deeper into our cultural values, social structures, or institutional arrangements as sources of poverty and human neglect. Having placed the blame, problems of class inequality need no longer concern us.

I would like to place "victim blaming" in the larger context of Empathy Failure, which is our learned inability to empathize with the victims of social injustice and inequality. And I use the term "learned" because there are so few social supports or opportunities for people to develop empathetic consciousness. If our more natural response is to empathize with the plight of fellow human beings, in our culture we must *learn* not to. In a society of winners and losers, we are taught to emulate the winners and avoid the losers. Whatever charitable impulses we might have toward losers is channelled into support for organizations such as United Way or even government welfare programs—as long as they don't cost too much. In effect, "charitable work" is meant to take care of the losers and mitigate against the worst excesses of a highly competitive system.

This sort of attitude, as pervasive as it is today, is not conducive to a productive society and it is probably inimical to some of America's traditions of democratic opportunity. The performance ethic in the economy and in education, and its attendant emphasis on supposedly objective screening of who gets ahead, has resulted in an unnecessary and unproductive structure of winners and losers. Unlike the past, however, the losers are dangerously close to becoming a permanent class, defying the dream in America that losers can eventually catch up and become winners. When degrees, diplomas and test scores become the criteria for allocating privilege, credential inflation threatens the morality of our system.

If we are to live up to democratic ideals and meet the practical realities of the world we live in, we must reward and encourage real productivity and resourcefulness. We cannot permit the credential spiral to continue unabated. A compassionate response to the losers requires us to reexamine our economic and educational institutions and how we allocate careers and positions of leadership. A system of winners and losers can no longer guarantee the economic and political future of our society.

Chapter 5

Toward a New Vision
The Emergence of the Productive Self

As American society faces the decade of the 1990s and immediately thereafter a new century, certain choices about our future are now possible. We can continue to be shaped by the performance ethic, living a half-life of measured conformity. Or we can begin to press for fundamental changes in cultural orientation and value in the hope of arriving at a new kind of selfhood, one that is less conformist and measured, a self that is more authentic and genuinely free.

I would like to offer two visions of self- and cultural orientation in America, presented as two options for the future of American life. The Present Vision encourages a selfhood I've been calling the Measured Self, formed as a response to the demands of the performance ethic. The New Vision refers to the productive self, and is shaped by an emerging cultural orientation that we can call the Productive Ethic, an idea similar to the Productive Orientation suggested by Erich Fromm some time ago.[1]

Toward a New Vision

The Present Vision

In the present, American character and personality is influenced heavily by a cultural performance ethic that produces all sorts of standards for human assessment and measurement, and the measured self is a direct outgrowth of the performance culture. It is an identity and sense of self expressed in performance terms — how well one is doing on a host of measured competencies, statuses and traits.

Using a developmental approach we saw the workings of the performance ethic on the lives of toddlers and their parents. We examined the pressure on young children to perform well at early ages on developmental tasks, growth activities and standardized tests, grades, aptitude assessments, etc. Parents of young children were portrayed as willing victims of the performance culture as their anxiety increased about their parenting skills. In seeing to it that their children measure up to myriad psychological, educational and developmental norms, parents push and prod their offspring to show signs of future success and potential. Following the dictates and lead of the educational system, parents motivate children to perform well in activities that can be objectively measured, and thus are capable of comparison with others.

Growing up in a culture dominated by the performance ethic, young people and adolescents are virtually robbed of their youth and innocence as the pressures to conform to quantified standards increase with each passing year. Since school life shapes so much of the identity of youth in our culture, measures of educational success, aptitude and achievement set the standards of normalcy and adjustment among the young. Adolescents are thus less free to set their own life agendas, to explore their own interests and values and to define their own purposes. Navigating their lives in a performance culture that permits little latitude for error or failure, young people must meet the externally imposed standards of a vastly extended school system (in the form of grades, test scores, etc.) if they hope to succeed in the work settings they will face as adults.

Moreover, young people find little respite from their overly-structured and school-saturated lives in the hedonistic peer group activities toward which they inevitably gravitate. For the peer group itself is heavily inundated with mass culture and consumerism and fails to provide a haven for young people from the performance pressures of school. Instead, peer group life centers around another highly competitive arena of fashion, looks, coolness and popularity. Caught between the paralyzing effects of the peer subculture and the performance pressure generated by the school system, many young people face the uncomfortable reality of not measuring up in either. Looking for any kind of recognition and acceptance in a culture that demands some sort of measured success, these youth may well seek acceptance in marginal groups where drug and alcohol abuse are acceptable forms of coping.

Adults in their middle years find that performance pressures can be most severe and produce the most desperate expression of the measured self. It is in the middle years that adults are expected to prove they have what it takes to measure up as men and women, spouses and parents, and as career-oriented people. Having neither their future before them as they did in their youth, nor past accomplishments to boast about as they might when older, adults in the middle years realize that only a few short years are theirs to accomplish and achieve all that the performance culture requires of them. The adult years, especially for those persons in the middle and professional class, are fraught with the anxieties attendant in achieving success in several areas of life. Often the success norms are contradictory and unrealistic, if not impossible.

Witness the dilemma of the contemporary, middle-class "complete" woman, who is trying to live up to the demands of her gender to be a sexy, slim, attractive wife, and an involved, caring parent to her children, all the while meeting the performance demands of the career she has chosen. Such women must deal with the anxiety of "completeness," of measuring up to competing and contradictory demands. Being a sexy, slim wife might mean devoting more time to the exercise spa than to PTA meetings, to say nothing of whether she should forego spending longer hours at the office necessary to look good for her next promotion.

Middle-class males as well experience the contradictory pressures of being aggressive, competitive males in the economic arena, striving for upward career mobility and financial success, yet somehow living up to new standards of parenthood as they attempt to give "quality time" to their children. In their desperate quest to "have it all," middle-class men often face the reality that, as males, economic success is the only true measure of their self-worth.

And finally, we have seen how the performance ethic in education and the workplace has resulted in an overcredentialed society, in which diplomas and degrees and test scores become the major screening devices for allocating economic and educational privilege. Performance on ostensibly neutral and objective criteria becomes a major determinant of who gets what in America. This supposedly meritocratic system masks the underlying class, ethnic and race inequalities that continue to exist in our society. The result is that Americans soon learn to blame the losers in the performance struggle, for, after all, the poor and the uneducated are at fault for failing to measure up to performance norms. Thus the poor are held responsible for their failure to obtain good grades, to score high on objective tests and to demonstrate academic potential and aptitude. The performance culture allows winners to take pride in the fact that their success was due to their educational merits and objective abilities, while citing the losers

Productive Self

for their lack of ability. One of the most damaging aspects of the performance ethic in education and economy is that it has led to a successful masking of the deeper causes of class, race and ethnic inequalities in America.

Moreover, the spiral of credentials means that increasing emphasis will be placed on credentials even more difficult to obtain for economic success. As whites and males of the middle and professional class continue to enjoy the benefits of educational privilege (college and professional school), they will secure for themselves the greatest economic privilege. We witnessed in the 1980s the emergence of an underclass, in danger of being permanently mired in an educational system that discriminates against them on test scores and grades, and an economic system that shuts them out from the more favored positions on the basis of credentials. The underclass is caught in a vicious performance struggle in which their failure to measure up educationally seals their economic fate. And while this process takes on the appearance of meritocracy, this system continues to favor affluent white males who usually end up winners.

Summary

The Present Vision is characterized by a measured self that results from a cultural orientation emphasizing measured performance. The measured self is dependent on the judgment of others (peer groups, teachers, parents, bosses, etc.); it is a selfhood that occasionally becomes nearly comfortable. For it is interesting to note today that beauty pageants never lack for entrants; organizational leaders willingly submit to all sorts of assessments and evaluations; diet, fitness and beauty magazines sell by the millions; and the Educational Testing Service at Princeton continues to thrive and prosper.

In a selfhood that is dependent on the judgment of others, a

Toward a New Vision

personality type emerges that is passive, conformist and anxious for approval. People are less likely to trust their own experiences and judgments; somehow their personal and unique habits, traditions and experiences are suspect and not highly valued. Inner feelings and voices are not regarded as authentic and meaningful compared to the objective and imposed standards of peer groups, organizations and the media. There results an exaltation of the external in which gender stereotypes are accepted as meaningful and real; grades and test scores become equated with education; and expert advice in the fields of psychology, medicine and even astrology are regarded as synonymous with sound personal judgment.

Rooted in certain twentieth century phenomena such as consumerism, bureaucratic rationality, scientism and professionalism, the performance ethic took shape as a major cultural orientation of our time. The measured self became a model character trait of the present, reaching its culmination in the 1980s, a decade characterized by mass consumerism, credentialism and professionalism. Many persons in American society might be comfortable in the measured self and its alienating aspects offer the haunting prospect that people can be secure in their unfreedom. Such was the vision so aptly described by Erich Fromm in his work on alienation and freedom.[2]

Despite the possibility that many people learn to find some sense of comfort and security in the measured self, I think it is worthwhile to explore a new vision of personality and cultural orientation in the decades to come. It is especially worth the effort to explore a personality type that offers people a more authentic existence, a deeper and more meaningful sense of self and new ways of relating to themselves, others and the external world.

Productive Self

A New Vision

I feel that the present is ripe with the possibility of imagining some new ways of being, thinking and acting. What these new alternatives might be is open to speculation, but it is fitting that I close this book by offering my insights into the direction that some of these changes might take.

Changes in cultural orientations and character come very slowly and haltingly, but it is worth envisioning new forms of selfhood if Americans in the nineties and beyond are going to be more genuinely free and at liberty to live the kinds of lives that make them more fully human. An agenda for the nineties must include new ways of looking at ourselves as parents, teachers, workers, and even more broadly as men and women.

I would like to set out the possibilities and potentials of a new sense of selfhood in America that I will call the "productive self." The identification here is built upon and extends the idea of the "productive orientation" developed by Erich Fromm in his book, *The Sane Society*.[3] But I'm not speaking here as much about a cultural orientation as I am about a kind of selfhood, a way of reorienting how Americans see themselves, and the kind of persons we could become. Cultural orientation is included to be sure, for much of selfhood is derived from culture. I'm describing the productive self not only as a form of orientation, but as a new possibility for people to be more fully human and less alienated. The productive self will refer to a life defined by each person's ability to release the creative, productive resources that lie within them. The productive self will draw more on inner sources of direction, action and creativity that can unleash a greater sense of human freedom and liberation.

Toward a New Vision

The Productive Self

In the material that follows, my thinking has benefitted greatly from the early work of Erich Fromm, who once argued that the solution to human alienation is productive activity.[4] I consider Fromm's theory as valid and fresh today as it was in the 1950s, and suggest that modern social critics and planners would do well to read carefully Fromm's criteria for a sane society.

People in America, as elsewhere, have a deep-seated need to engage in their world productively and actively. Humans are creative and they need to express that creativity in much if not all that they do. The productive self wants to shape and build, and at the same time to see something of the self in the world that is being formed. The productive self desires a more direct and tangible connection between effort and value; actions are taken because they are possible and worthwhile and in touch with human wants and needs. At whatever age in life, regardless of gender, race or class, people fundamentally desire to live and work productively in freedom. The productive self is actualized in building and creating the world, not in merely reacting to external demands and conformity pressures, or in seeking approval. Whereas the measured self is passive, reactive, approval-oriented and mistrustful of its own judgments and experiences, the productive self is active, inner-directed, self-reliant and constructive.

How can we give shape and substance to this productive self? Where are changes in American culture most necessary to allow the productive self to nurture and flourish? In three institutions of American society: family, education and economy/work.

Family

There is a certain danger in generalizing about family life in America, as well as in thinking that only one type of family exists.

Productive Self

For in fact, we know there is no single type of American family, thus admonitions about the future of the "family" are both suspicious and inaccurate. Recognizing this and limiting my remarks essentially to the middle-class and professional class in America, I would like to probe into new directions and emphases for family life.

Christopher Lasch, in his description of family life in Western society, provides about the best analysis of the demise of parenting in the modern world.[5] Arguing that just as the industrial revolution and new theories of scientific management devalued the knowledge and skills of workers, so did industrialism extend control over people's private lives as medical, psychological and educational experts began to devalue the knowledge and skills of parents. "The proliferation of medical and psychiatric advice undermines parental confidence at the same time that it encourages a vastly inflated idea of the importance of child-rearing techniques and of the parents' responsibility for their failure."[6] Nowhere is this more in evidence today than in middle-class America. Parents are often frantic in their desire to parent according to the latest models and to instill in their children the motivation to succeed and achieve.

Trusting neither in their own intuitions or experiences, middle-class parents become nearly completely other-directed, approval-oriented, dependent and anxious. Fearing they will fail themselves as they fail their children, they anxiously await the latest pronouncements of pediatricians, psychiatrists and child-guidance experts. Is it any wonder that their children become so approval-oriented, conformist and anxious about their own abilities? How can children become productive and resourceful and confident in their own creative capabilities, when their parents have so little confidence in their own?

In reading through a variety of books giving advice on child-rearing, I had two reactions. One, there is an overabundance of

Toward a New Vision

information about techniques, skills and approaches in raising children. There is enough to confuse rather than clarify. But I was also struck by the idea that much of the expert, detailed advice could be distilled into a few basic ideas. For it seems important to most advice-givers that parents should treat their children with respect, encourage open communication, employ firm discipline and give lots of encouragement. These suggestions hardly appear to be so esoteric, scientific, or complex that the average parent couldn't grasp them.

In fact, these basic components of parenting are quite consistent with a more productive orientation toward parenting and childhood itself. What is implied here is that parents, in establishing a sense of mutual respect, are in effect allowing children to engage in their own maturing, permitting them to grow, create and build something of themselves and for themselves in a world where they feel secure, cared for, important and respected. Such an environment is not all that difficult to establish, and is no doubt within the competencies of most mature adults.

Despite the information in countless magazines, advice columns and books, modern parents do not have to be all things to their children; there is no one "correct" method of raising children, and parents cannot be held all that responsible for their children's outcomes. Moreover, there is nothing healthy or constructive in any formula that guarantees success in raising children to achieve.

The trap is that in the present vision dominated by the performance ethic, successful parenting is nearly synonymous with raising children to be achievement oriented. Parents are admonished to nurture their children to make good, especially in ways that can be objectively measured and compared, such as grades, test scores, batting averages, etc.

In the new vision, where the productive ethic is encouraged and the productive self is allowed to flourish, parenting-for-

Productive Self

success isn't the ultimate goal of parenting, nor is it all that necessary that parents learn the scientific techniques for motivating their children. Assuming that the need to be productively engaged in the world is inherent in all humans, and I believe it is, in the new vision all that is required of parents is that they provide an environment that is secure, respectful, communicative, encouraging and disciplined. Whether or not children succeed and measure up is not that relevant. What is important is that children are allowed the freedom to find some reflection of who they are and what they are becoming as they engage the world. For some children this might be finding themselves in activities that the school systems reward, while other children might pursue less conventional avenues that cannot readily be labeled. But this should not mean that one has failed and the other has measured up. The less conventional avenues might permit as much self-discovery, self-mastery and creativity as the activities that the school systematically rewards.

Parents, in providing a productive, secure environment can trust their own intuitive and experiential skills as adults without worrying that they will fail. In the new vision, parents need not be all things to their children. It is enough that they are there, present in the environment in which their children are growing. Their children in turn will grow on their own terms, at their own pace, according to their own capacities and strengths. I think it is enough for parents to accept themselves and their children in their essential humanness. Whether children "achieve" is another matter.

Earlier we learned from Sheila Kitzinger that while the entire context of family life has changed in industrial societies, modern parents still have things to learn from their counterparts in peasant and pre-industrial societies.[7] Though referring mainly to the mothering role, Kitzinger reminds modern parents that children have been raised for centuries in peasant societies without the aid of modern psychiatric and medical authority. Relying essentially on traditional, folk and community wisdom, mothers raised their offspring by following village norms. By eschewing most if not all of the advice so readily doled out by modern "experts on the child," contemporary parents may enjoy some of the advantages of parents in peasant communities.

Finally, it is instructive in this context to review the findings of the Goertzels in their studies of "eminence."[8] Persons who have risen to eminence in the modern world were not those raised by model parents, nor were they raised "by the book." In fact, for many of the eminent, their early family environment was anything but happy, and their parents often failed in their attempts to be positive role models. Many creative people did not come from warm, supportive homes. Parents of eminent persons were often eccentric, nonconformist, troubled and socially deviant. However, in many of the homes of the eminent, learning was a respected as well as *creative* endeavor. Interesting also is the fact that in many homes of the eminent, fathers read to their children.

The pattern in eminence appears to be strong-willed, opinionated parents who pretty much followed their own inclinations and prejudices in raising their children. Perhaps there is a lesson here for modern, middle-class parents who feel compelled to consult expert advice at nearly every turn of their children's "development." Perhaps children's natural creative and productive abilities will take root and be stimulated in a family environment less saturated by scientific theories of child-rearing and more characterized by parents who feel free to be themselves and take delight in such relatively simple tasks as reading to their children.

The productive ethic in family life and parenting means creating environments in the home where the productive selves of children and adults are more free to emerge and take shape. Opportunities for creative and innovative play, work, building and producing are foundations for such an environment. A basic trust and respect for human differences and preferences is paramount in creating the environment in the family where all members are free to seek inner commitments and formulate their own plans for selfhood. As part of a family and parenting agenda for the nineties, it is time now to get beyond the Age of the Expert and the preeminence of scientific authority in family life.

Education

Nowhere is the need for a new vision of the productive self more evident than in the educational system. Nearly supplanting the family, the modern school is a major socializer of children. No child can escape the influence of the school, and how well children perform their school tasks will be a significant factor in determining their economic futures. American schools have become increasingly important in shaping children's identities, how they see themselves and their definitions of self-worth. It is in the educational institution that the possibilities of a new vision of the productive self are most crucial, yet I recognize that this very institution could be the most impervious to change. But change it we must if we are to allow our children greater freedom and self-direction in their lives.

There have been many criticisms of contemporary schooling in America and it's not my intention to review them here. However, the works of authors Bowles and Gintis, and Ivan Illich are especially relevant.

Bowles and Gintis in their work *Schooling in Capitalist America* do much to explode the myth of the meritocratic function of modern education.[9] Their data amply document that the educational system in our society is not based on true meritocratic selection, but exists primarily to legitimize economic inequality. They argue that educational meritocracy is mostly symbolic, and

Toward a New Vision

that schooling does little to improve the chances for the poor and racial and ethnic minorities to succeed.

Bowles and Gintis cite evidence as well that schools tend to reward docility, passivity and obedience. Students exhibiting these traits tend to do better in school, get higher grades and win approval from teachers. In fact, traits such as creativity and spontaneity tend to be penalized. Those students most approval-oriented and measurement-conscious are most highly valued and rewarded by teachers. Such an environment encourages school-age children to adopt the measured self as their best chance of success.

No one has leveled more devastating and convincing criticism at modern schooling than Ivan Illich, who argues that schooling fails precisely because it links instruction with certification.[10] Diplomas and degrees become the essential prizes of education. Persons with the most degrees, who have been instructed the longest, are assumed to be the "most educated." Illich contends that nothing could be further from the truth.

"In school we are taught that valuable learning is the result of attendance; that the value of learning increases with the amount of input; and, finally that the value can be measured and documented by grades and certificates."[11] Most real learning, however, takes place by "doing and acting" in a setting, Illich argues — not necessarily by institutionalized planning. Lamentably, once societies accept the idea of schooling, all other forms of knowledge and learning are rejected.

Illich also criticizes schools for perpetuating the "myth of measurement of values." Young people are taught that everything can be measured, even their imaginations and their humanity.

School pretends to break learning up into subject "matters" to build into the pupil a curriculum made of prefabricated blocks and to gauge the result on an international scale.

Productive Self

People who submit to the standard of others for the measure of their own personal growth soon apply the same rule to themselves. They no longer have to be put in their place, but put themselves into their assigned slots, squeeze themselves into the niche which they have been taught to seek, and, in the very process, put their fellows into their places too, until everybody and everything fits.[12]

In a schooled society, says Illich, what can't be measured becomes secondary and threatening. Schools thus become the primary arena of measuring-up activities, education proliferates with grading systems, test scores, aptitude quotients, popularity ratings, etc. Young people are eventually inured to all these processes of measurement. The myth of the measurement of values leads ultimately to the competitive nature of schools, in which school-age children are constantly competing with each other for grades, test scores and other forms of approval. School systems by their very nature create categories of "winners and losers."

Children with natural impulses toward creativity, spontaneity and curiosity soon learn to curb them, or suffer the label of being a misfit or troublemaker. And the school-age peer group is no haven for students seeking a respite from measuring-up activities. The modern peer group is firmly attached to the requirements of consumerism, and the competition for fashions, electronic gadgets, etc. among the young is nearly as severe as competition for grades.

Is there the possibility of a new vision in education, that would encourage a more productive ethic in learning and give shape to the productive self in young learners? I think that there is, and it is helpful to turn to the new educational visions being developed by alternative school advocates and some of the tenets of holistic education.

Toward a New Vision

To begin with, we need to decide what kind of learning experiences we want young people to have in a world that is complex and changing. In examining the new models for learning, two themes emerge that challenge the traditional views of education. The first theme builds on the idea that a cooperative ethic must replace the competitive ethic in education; the second suggests that not all important learning is measurable.

Thomas Lasley and John Bregenzer recently set up a model for schooling based on "selflessness."[13] Using a series of propositions, these two educators argue that cooperation in schools is possible and will lead to a more productive learning environment than the traditional competitive model.

For example, Lasley and Bregenzer propose that schools emphasize group welfare over individual welfare. Such an emphasis would move away from ranking systems that hamper a sense of community among students and teachers. Citing how simple cultures promote the idea of community problem-solving, this process lessens the pressure on individuals to compete and succeed. Cooperation can be learned and reinforced within the right environment, and schools, using the model of simple cultures, can create such environments. These authors suggest that modern school systems suffer from too much hierarchy; education is inevitably an exercise in authority. By promoting a sense of community in schools, students and staff are able to establish common goals and purposes, breaking down the authority barriers that hamper real learning.

Moreover, Lasley and Bregenzer suggest that involvement replace isolation in schools. One of the educational practices in modern schools that leads to isolation is the use of ability groups based on test scores. Ability groups heighten competition, and students in the lower ability groups experience a sense of isolation, defeat and loss of self-worth.

Educator William Pink, who has studied the effects of teach-

Productive Self

ing systems and ability groups for many years, argues that ability grouping as an educational method has some serious side-effects.[14] Low status groups develop a negative self-image among students; often they become disillusioned with school. In many cases the disillusionment can result in anti-social behavior during school hours. If the deviant behavior is severe enough, students may be encouraged to leave school, blaming themselves for their failure. Those students who drop out have very limited life options in a credential-oriented society.

Competition in education produces isolation and reduces a sense of mutuality among students. Without a sense of shared responsibility students become ego-centered, and those students who perform well tend to lack any compassionate response toward those students who don't measure up.

Finally, Lasley and Bregenzer contend that one of the most important lessons students can learn in schools is a sense of responsibility. Students must learn to be accountable for their actions. Students not only have a responsibility to themselves but a responsibility to their fellow students and community. Interestingly, these authors suggest that one of the most effective ways to promote a feeling of responsibility among students is to give them experiences in caring for and nurturing others. They argue that the modern household has virtually eliminated chores — young people don't carry out productive work around the house to help the family survive. Children are robbed of their opportunity to contribute to the welfare of their most immediate communities. Schools can create the feeling of community responsibility in students by allowing them to perform nurturing activities with and for others. As an illustration, several alternative schools in the United States require students to do volunteer work in the community, working in nursing homes, day-care centers, etc.[15] All of this can be viewed as part of productive learning.

Toward a New Vision

To summarize the first theme in a new vision of education: cooperation must replace competition in schools. Grade competition produces a hostile learning environment in which too many students feel isolated and second-class. Competing for grades leads to over-conformity and encouragement for a selfhood among students that is approval oriented and self-centered.

Cooperative models in education, on the other hand, reward and encourage group problem-solving and group processes. By encouraging group problem-solving the sense of community is strengthened. With less pressure for individual grades, students don't feel so anxious about having to measure up continually. When group efforts are emphasized, students learn to accept responsibility for their behavior and they develop more compassionate responses to their fellow students. As students become more comfortable in a less competitive environment, they might well have less need to form the rigid, conformist types of peer groups that now characterize the modern school setting. While peer groups will still flourish in a productive and cooperative learning environment, the peer group could extend and encourage better relations among students.

This cooperative-group approach in education is really more consistent with the newer styles of management being employed in industry and work in America. Allowing students greater opportunities for group problem-solving in the schools gives them important presocialization into organizational and work environments.

The second theme in contemporary education that we need to address as part of the new vision for a productive self is the fact that not all important learning is measurable. I would like to borrow from the thinking of Edward Clark, who speaks about a "new educational paradigm."[16]

Clark contends that the field of education is gradually undergoing a shift based on an ecological point of view. This emerging view is holistic, global and integrative, in contrast to the old educational paradigm that stressed linear sequential thinking.

According to Clark, the old assumptions in education assumed that children were born with a determined, measurable and quantifiable amount of intelligence. This assumption justified all the testing carried out in the schools to determine the intellectual capability of each student. Under the new paradigm, the assumption is that each child has innate potential for learning that simply cannot be quantified.

Several generations of teachers have been trained to teach solely on the basis of instructional and behavioral objectives. For the most part, things were taught so that students' learning could be demonstrated and quantified. As a result, teachers taught only those things that could generate measurable results.

Clark directs us to a new educational paradigm based on recent scientific discoveries about the ways human beings think and recognize the world. The new paradigm in education must include these assumptions: all children do not learn the same way, therefore it is both futile and counter-productive to standardize and measure numerically what is learned. Likewise, all learning begins with what Clark refers to as a "context," a large mental picture of something. Clark argues that the human brain gropes for a context or image as the beginning of all thinking. In the old paradigm, teachers anxiously tried to break things up and reduce them to their smallest parts; under the new paradigm students are encouraged to begin with complete or contextual thinking and images. This is part of what Clark and others refer to as holistic education, or whole-brain thinking and imaging. Using all parts of thinking, even intuition and feelings, encourages students to grasp the totality of problems and ideas.

It is interesting to contrast here holistic thinking with the grading systems of schools operating under the old paradigm. A grading system forces teachers to measure really only a small part

Toward a New Vision

of what has been learned. Persons with exceptional ability and who desire contextual thinking and imaging are not motivated in this way. This is one of the reasons geniuses and visionaries usually don't do well in school, or like schooling. Henry Ford and Albert Einstein are cases in point, holistic thinkers who had relatively undistinguished careers as students and resented the constraints that a grading system imposed on them.[17] The intellectual "gift" that Einstein and Ford possessed was their ability to see the world and to solve problems in ways that stood outside the current thinking of their day. They relied heavily on intuition, on holistic and integrative thinking, as they imagined the working of the world they were presented with. Very little of the kind of thinking Ford and Einstein engaged in could be objectively measured according to grades or test scores. That these two men revolutionized the fields of industrial manufacturing and physics had as much to do with how they thought as it did with their genius. (And I don't mean here to downplay Einstein's extraordinary intellectual powers.) As holistic thinkers Ford and Einstein created new visions for the world, and Clark contends that encouraging holistic thinking among all students can have similar, if less dramatic, results.

While few, if any, students will be Einstein's intellectual equal, students can be stimulated to use much more of their brain and imagination than they currently use. It is in this sense that Clark argues that individuals have enormous learning potentials untapped by schools and beyond present measurement. In Clark's words, "We have reduced concepts like understand, know, appreciate, enjoy, and believe, into measurable behaviors like write, recite, identify, list, compose, and contrast."[18]

In a new vision in education based on the ideas of Clark, Lasley, Bergenzer and many others involved in holistic and alternative education, the possibilities of productive activity in learning are becoming more evident. Children might begin to relish

Productive Self

school when they are encouraged in contextual thinking and group problem-solving. As children cherish their educational experiences they will be less likely to drop out or cause trouble and schools might be less expensive to maintain. When students' learning allows them to actively engage the world, to use their entire brain, and when their intuitions and feelings are affirmed and rewarded, school can be an arena where the productive self can flourish. Under the present vision, we tend to confuse evaluation with education and have forced young people into rigid systems of competition, stratification and conformity. Such a system is neither in their best interests as young learners, nor is it in the best interests of a society in which global problem-solving and adaptation require more flexible and productive systems of learning and thinking. We need a generation of young people who can think, interpret and work cooperatively as they envision new possibilities for the world.

Economy/Work

Some years ago, Ivan Illich argued that modern machine technology no longer worked for people but tended to enslave them.[19] While technology is usually developed to meet a human problem (medicine, transportation, etc.), the eventual production of technology leads to bureaucratic control. Instead of freeing people to lead more productive lives, technology often produces processes of control and management that make people less creative and less in control of their lives.

Illich proposes a more "people oriented" technology that would give them more control over their production. Referring to this new technology as "convivial tools," Illich hoped to counteract the human devastation caused by destructive tools that increase regimentation, exploitation and impotence. Convivial tools promote more human freedom because they allow more

Toward a New Vision

autonomous and creative intercourse among persons. Such tools will bring people together, and give them greater freedom from the rules and management of experts. Illich argues that science has made most tools too complex for individual use—therefore people must rely excessively on professionals and authorities. Illich would have science do the opposite. By simplifying tools, lay persons can use them to give shape and meaning to their environments. As it now stands, industrialization places exaggerated emphasis on standardized products, uniform processes and certified quality. Illich laments that in such an industrial model the distinction between a personal vocation and standard profession becomes blurred.

Illich's argument is compelling and prophetic, though it must be admitted that the concept of "convivial tools" is sufficiently vague and hazy to allow little practical reform in work and technology. Illich is never able to fully describe what it would take to bring about a convivial society or to share with us a clear and realistic vision of what convivial tools are and how they are to be used.

However, his critique of modern technology and work is to the point, and refreshing. The goals of any economic and technological system cannot be limited to control, standardization and management efficiency, even if, in the short run, the result is financial profitability. The human goal of work is to be productively engaged; people want to work in ways that maximize their ability to see themselves in what they do and that allow them some real sense of accomplishment. People need meaningful work they can feel good about, that contributes to their sense of well-being and their need to be creatively engaged.

Under the present vision, the measured self is the result of an economic/work system that reveres only measurable results (income, promotion, etc.), that promotes excessive competition and power struggles between genders, that contributes to demeaning gender stereotyping. Instead of adult men and women finding their life's significance in creative and meaningful work, they are often trapped in a dehumanizing struggle to obtain the commercial and material trappings of success. And success standards are externally imposed and constantly shifting due to the ebb and flow of events on Wall Street and Madison Avenue. Rather than being free to choose the most productive and creative avenues to fulfillment, adults pursue the most socially approved lines of gender and status conformity.

Moreover, the performance ethic in the present vision leads to excessive reliance on credentials in allocating rewards and privileges. Credentialing is used to insure the privilege of some groups and to keep other groups in relatively permanent positions of poverty and unemployment. American society can be characterized as a system of winners and losers, with the losers slipping further behind in the credential race, their realistic chances of finding any kind of success and dignified work in the present economy increasingly slim.

Is it possible that in the decades to come we can create an economic structure that will allow people to lead more productive and meaningful work lives and at the same time distribute economic and social justice more equally? Or are these goals somehow incompatible?

I would like to argue that the nineties can witness the emergence of the productive self in economy and work and at the same time create greater opportunities for the poor and minorities to enjoy the fruits of a productive life as well. And I am not alone in my thinking. Recent literature on America's economic/work future draws similar conclusions. I would like to review just a couple of the recent work models being proposed.

Robert Reich is one commentator who attests that American society stands on the verge of a "new frontier" in economics and work.[20] This new frontier, if we choose to enter it, will assure

Toward a New Vision

greater human productivity and engagement at the same time it addresses the dilemma of economic justice. His argument deserves close attention.

Reich contends that heretofore America's production system was based on "high volume standard production" and all previous management theory was guided by that. Under the "old management system" work goals were to break complex tasks down into simple ones, to devise fixed rules governing the work process itself and to monitor carefully worker output (especially relying on quantified monitoring systems). Reich maintains that such a management system was functional in America during previous decades when America dominated world markets and international competition was not very threatening.

However, since the 1970s global competition has increased dramatically; the American economy has suffered because Third World countries can do "high volume" production much more cheaply. The Third World can draw from a large supply of inexpensive labor, and America finds itself hard-pressed to compete.

Reich argues that America can no longer rely exclusively on the high volume economy and hope to enjoy prosperity in the nineties and beyond. Rather, management philosophy must shift to the "flexible system" approach which stresses teamwork and group cooperation. This is especially appropriate in an economic era characterized by rapidly changing technologies and greater demand for custom service products. In view of the latter requirements, the traditional management system is hopelessly outmoded.

In the flexible system production of the new frontier much of the training for work will be gained by on-the-job experience. Since precise skills and abilities cannot always be anticipated, educational credentials won't or shouldn't count as much. Cooperative effort will become increasingly important in flexible sys-

Productive Self

tems since much of the custom service will be produced through work groups. Persons in work groups will be required to learn each other's capabilities and to be interchangeable. Product quality will be as important as quantity, and since quality is not as easily measurable, traditional monitoring systems will decrease in importance. In large part, quality will be assured by groups working together and encouraged to be creative and spontaneous in response to problems. Workers will need more "inner" commitment to product quality rather than being satisfied to measure up to externally imposed standards of output.

The "flexible system" of the nineties is also compatible with the calls for justice from those persons who have been left out in an overly credentialed and overly competitive economic system. Reich shares these thoughts:

> ... in the emerging order of productivity, social justice is not incompatible with economic growth, but essential to it. A social organization premised on equity, security, and participation will generate greater productivity than one premised on greed and fear. Collaboration and collective adaptation are coming to be more important in an industrialized nation's well-being than are personal daring and ambition. And at an even more fundamental level, the goals of prosperity and social justice cannot be validly separated.[21]

One final problem in American management that Reich addresses is the traditional quest for short-term profits. In the past, American management has been under pressure to create profits in order to appease higher-level management, to guarantee good returns to investors and to attract new investors. This situation has produced, according to Reich, a short-term perspective on the part of managers as they seek to measure up and define their success according to the "bottom line" at the end of each quarter or year. One outcome of this process is the emergence of "paper entrepreneurialism" — in which managers are basically making paper adaptations and manipulations to produce profits.[22] The recent spate of mergers, acquisitions and buy-outs among America's corporations are cases in point. Reich asserts that such entrepreneurialism does not create any new wealth (thus more jobs and economic opportunities) but merely rearranges industrial assets.

Under the present vision where the performance ethic proliferates, American managers can hardly do otherwise. So long as managerial success continues to be objectively and quantifiably measured and profits and returns on assets are the only criteria of management evaluation, the short-term perspective will remain entrenched. Only under the new vision, where the productive ethic is given highest value, will management be free to make decisions based on the potential of people and enterprises, not merely on the basis of profit. As Reich notes, successful economies currently are those that eschew the short-term profit in favor of long-term investments in human and industrial productivity. Good management will be rewarded for productivity gains, not simply for year-end profit statements.

Finally, we are faced with the dilemmas associated with an over credentialed society in which millions of poor and minorities have few realistic possibilities to be productively engaged. Solutions here are exceedingly complex and it would be beyond our scope to provide a blueprint for long-range change. Long-term solutions will probably emerge only with a major overhaul of our economy, which in the future may guarantee to all people the right to dignified, productive work and a secure environment.

In the short run other avenues to assist the underclass can be suggested. If Reich is correct that in the future "flexible" management systems will predominate and most experience will be gained on the job, then this alone could do much to reduce the importance our economy attaches to educational credentials, grades, etc. Quite possibly those persons lacking advanced educational credentials will be given greater opportunities to prove their talents on the job. Very recent evidence by sociologist David Bills shows this may currently be the case in some organizations.[23] His research into hiring and promoting practices in six organizations shows that educational credentials are used more for hiring from outside than promoting within. Bills implies that once a person is hired, it is the on-the-job experience that is the greatest asset in promotion.

Consider Reich's contention that flexible management systems will give greater importance to group cooperation, teamwork and problem-solving. In light of this, the educational strategies being formulated by holistic educators and leaders in the alternative education movement are probably on the right track. It is precisely the cooperative models in education, not the competitive ones, that will give young people the greatest advantage in flexible management systems. By deemphasizing grades, standardized tests, etc., minorities might do just as well as whites. When cooperative models are employed, and excessive competition becomes outmoded, greater numbers of minorities may finish their education and have enough group and team experiences in problem-solving to make them initially attractive to employers.

All of this, of course, remains for the future. Unfortunately, public education today is under such pressure to produce better educational "results" that school leaders have difficulty seeing beyond holding students up to greater measurable accountability. Thus, some states have initiated more testing of standardized competence, not less. True educational reform in America's schools will only begin when the connections between the flexible management systems and cooperative learning models are made more explicit.

Toward a New Vision

In a recent book, *The New Social Contract*, the authors suggest that the government can be an employer of the disadvantaged, if private-sector priorities continue to leave so many poor and minorities unemployed.[24] Shearer, Carnoy and Rumsberger argue that the government is a major employer in our society anyway, employing fully one-sixth of the American work force. The government has generated one-fourth of all the new jobs in the economy over the last two decades. Government employment benefits women and minorities as well; discrimination in earnings for these two groups is much less in government work than in the private sector.

Calling for greater public investment, these authors point to the tremendous need today to rebuild America's roads, bridges, mass transit systems, etc. They also note that government is often no less efficient than giant corporations, and given the record of fairness to women and minorities it could well be that government hiring is the answer to the problems of the underclass, at least in the short run. Since much of the underclass is trapped in urban ghettos that are themselves in great need of rebuilding, perhaps government employment and greater public investment in the urban environment are the most immediate and efficient solutions to the poverty and despair of the underclass. Maybe it's time to realize the private sector is simply not going to respond to the plight of the underclass, and we, as a society, can no longer afford to have millions unemployed, underemployed and nearly desperate in an economy that can't do much for them.

We all know there is much productive work to be done in America. Where private firms find it unprofitable, public institutions must find it necessary and vital, and begin securing jobs for people who need them.

In the long run, however, the traditional losers in our economic system are best served by a reorientation of our economic and work priorities. Human productivity, the unleashing of human

Productive Self

innovativeness and creativity in work situations must be given greater priority. We must begin to replace the often unproductive and dehumanizing effects of excessive profit orientation, and the constant monitoring and objective evaluation of performance in organizations. When experience replaces credentials, cooperation replaces competition, and ability to contribute to group productivity and problem-solving is given greater priority, perhaps, eventually, traditional distinctions between a credentialed elite and a noncredentialed underclass will begin to disappear. If real learning and enhanced human productivity are better served by greater cooperation and less emphasis on quantitative and objectively measured results, then both our economic and educational institutions will be strengthened.

The new vision of the productive self offers fresh possibilities of being, relatedness and productivity for Americans if we choose to reorient our values and self-definitions. The decade of the 1990s contains the promise of opportunities to redirect American culture and selfhood, to live more productively, cooperatively and meaningfully. We may well usher in a period when adults and children are less pressured to measure up to countless standards of competence, perfection, success and beauty, and more free to enter into productive and creative relations with others as they seek to build and live in a world more in their own image and to their own liking.

Notes

Introduction. Performance Ethic in American Culture

1. David Riesman, *The Lonely Crowd* (New Haven: Yale University Press, 1950).

Chapter 1. Measuring Up: The Early Years

1. Sheldon B. Korones, *High Risk Newborn Infants* (St. Louis: C. V. Mosby, 1981).
2. Philip Aries, *Centuries of Childhood* (New York: Alfred A. Knopf, 1962).
3. Ibid., p. 411.
4. David Elkind, *The Hurried Child* (Reading, Mass.: Addison-Wesley, 1981).
5. Glen Doman, *How to Multiply Your Baby's Intelligence* (New York: Doubleday, 1981). Burton Wite, *The First Three Years of Life* (Englewood Cliffs, New Jersey: Prentice-Hall, 1975).
6. Frances Ilg, Louise Bates, and Sidney Baker, *Child Development* (New York: Harper & Row, 1981).

Notes to Pages 20–46

7. Howard James, *Children in Trouble* (New York: David McKay, 1969).

8. Letty Pogrebin, "The Secret Fear That Keeps Us from Raising Free Children" in *Feminist Frontiers: Rethinking Sex, Gender and Society*, Laurel Richardson and Verta Taylor, eds. (Reading, Mass.: Addison-Wesley, 1983).

9. Barbara Ehrenreich, *The Hearts of Men* (Garden City: Anchor Press/Doubleday, 1983).

10. Brad Edmundson, "The Demographics of Guilt," *American Demographics*, March 1986, pp. 33–56.

11. Ibid., p. 33.

12. Ibid.

13. Barbara Ehrenreich and Dierdre English, *For Her Own Good* (Garden City: Anchor Press/Doubleday, 1979).

14. Christopher Lasch, *Haven in a Heartless World* (New York: Basic Books, 1977).

15. Sheila Kitzinger, *Women as Mothers* (New York: Vintage Books, 1978).

16. Ibid., p. 11.

17. John Seely, Alexander Sim, and Elizabeth Loosley, *Crestwood Heights* (New York: John Wiley, 1963).

18. "As Families Are Less Stable, Schools Inherit Responsibilities," *New York Times News Service*, 1986.

19. Kenneth Keniston, "11-Year-Olds of Today Are the Computer Terminals of Tomorrow," *New York Times*, February 19, 1976.

20. "Teaching in Trouble," *U.S. News & World Report*, May 26, 1986, p. 52.

21. For an excellent discussion of the problems in measuring human ability, see: Stephan Gould, *The Mismeasure of Man* (New York: W. W. Norton, 1981).

22. Victor Goertzel and Mildred Goertzel, *Cradles of Eminence* (Boston: Little, Brown, 1962).

23. Ibid., p. 130.

Chapter 2. Why Teens Try Harder: Adolescent Life in America

1. Charles E. Basch, Theresa B. Kersch, "Adolescent Perceptions of Stressful Life Events," *Health Education*, June/July 1986, pp. 4–7.
2. Jane Rinzler, *Teens Speak Out* (New York: Donald Fine, 1985).
3. R. L. Huenemann, et al., "A Longitudinal Study of Gross Body Composition and Body Conformation and Their Association with Food and Activity in a Teen-Age Population," *American Journal of Clinical Nutrition*, 18, 1966, pp. 325–338.
4. Jan Krukowski, "What Do Students Want? Status," *Change*, May/June 1985, pp. 21–28.
5. "Privileges of Prepping," *Newsweek*, January 20, 1986, pp. 56–58.
6. Ibid., p. 56.
7. David Elkind, "Stress and the Middle-Grader," *The School Counselor*, 33, January 1986, pp. 196–206.
8. David Owen, *None of the Above: Behind the Myth of Scholastic Aptitude* (Boston: Houghton-Mifflin, 1985).
9. Daniel T. Regan, *NCAA NEWS*, February 18, 1987.
10. "Treating Teens in Trouble," *Newsweek*, January 20, 1986, p. 52.
11. Ibid.
12. A. P. Schoff, "Drug Problems in Athletics—It's Not Only the Pros," *U.S. News and World Report*, October 17, 1983, pp. 164–66.
13. D. M. Garner, et al., "Cultural Expectations of Thinness in Women," *Psychological Reports*, 47, 1980, pp. 483–491.
14. Susie Orbach, *Hunger Strike: The Anorectic's Struggle as a Metaphor for Our Age* (New York: Norton, 1986).
15. Marlene Boskind-Lodahl, "Cinderella's Step-Sisters: A Feminist Perspective on Anorexia Nervosa and Bulimia," *Signs: A Journal of Women in Culture and Society*, 2, 1976, pp. 342–356.
16. "Teen Suicide: Two Death Pacts Shake the Country," *Time*, March 23, 1987, pp. 12–13.
17. Philip Slater, *The Pursuit of Loneliness* (Boston: Beacon Press, 1970).

18. Bruce Dykeman, "Adolescent Suicide: Recognition and Intervention," *College Student Journal*, Vol. 18, Winter 1984, pp. 364–368.
19. Emile Durkheim, *Suicide* (New York: The Free Press, 1966).
20. "The Copycat Suicides," *Newsweek*, March 23, 1987, pp. 28–29.
21. Quoted in Jan Krukowski, Ibid.
22. Ibid.
23. "Study Says Mergers are Leaving Many Students Unemployed," *Indiana Statesman*, January 13, 1987.
24. David L. Warren, "Pizza, Popcorn and the President," *Change*, May/June 1985, p. 29.
25. David Elkind, *All Grown Up and No Place to Go* (Reading, Mass.: Addison-Wesley, 1984).
26. "The Brain Battle," *U.S. News and World Report*, January 19, 1987, pp. 59–61.
27. Mamoru Iga, "Suicide of Japanese Youth," *Suicide and Life-Threatening Behavior*, Vol. 11, Spring 1981, pp. 17–31.

Chapter 3. The Measured Self in the Middle Years

1. *New York Magazine*, January 20, 1986.
2. *Mother Earth News*, March/April, 1986.
3. David Reisman, *The Lonely Crowd* (New Haven: Yale University Press, 1950).
4. Joe L. Dubbert, "Progressivism and the Masculinity Crisis" in *The American Man*, Elizabeth Pleck and Joseph Pleck, eds. (Englewood Cliffs: Prentice-Hall, 1980).
5. Peter Stearns, *Be a Man: Males in Modern Society* (New York: Holmes and Meier, 1979).
6. Paul Goodman, *Growing Up Absurd* (New York: Random House, 1962).
7. Marc Faigen Fasteau, *The Male Machine* (New York: McGraw-Hill, 1974).
8. *Ulrich's International Periodicals Directory* (24th Edition), (New York: R. R. Bowker, 1985).

9. Michael Farrell and Stanley Rosenberg, *Men at Midlife*, (Boston: Auburn House Publishing, 1981).
10. Michael Farrell and Stanley Rosenberg, "Male Midlife Decline" in *Men in Difficult Times*, Robert Lewis, ed.(Englewood Cliffs: Prentice-Hall, 1981).
11. Lois Tamir, *Men in Their Forties: The Transition to Middle Age*, (New York: Springer Publisher, 1982).
12. Steven Floris, quoted in *Common Cause Magazine*, March/April, 1985, p. 8.
13. Nancy Chodorow, *The Reproduction of Mothering* (Berkeley, University of California Press, 1978).
14. Susie Orbach, *Fat is a Feminist Issue* (New York: Berkley Publishers, 1984).
15. "Cross-Addiction: Surprising Results of the *Ms.* Survey," *Ms. Magazine*, February, 1987, pp. 44–47.
16. "Bias Against Ugly People," *U.S. News and World Report*, November 28, 1983, pp. 53–54.
17. Pete Hamill, "Great Expectations," *Ms. Magazine*, September, 1986, pp. 34–83.
18. Ibid., p. 37.
19. Carol Osborn, *Enough is Enough: Exploding the Myth of Having it All* (New York: F. P. Putnams, 1986).
20. Ibid., Hamill, p. 37.
21. Ibid., Hamill, p. 83.
22. Gail Sheehy, *Passages* (New York: Dutton, 1976).
23. Betty Lehan Harrogan, *Games Mother Never Taught You* (New York: Warner Books, 1977).
24. Jacqueline Landau and Lisa Amoss, "Myths, Dreams and Disappointments: Preparing Women for the Future" in *Not as Far as You Think*, Lynda Moore, ed. (Lexington: D.C. Heath, 1986).
25. "You've Come a Long Way, Baby—But Not as Far as You Thought," *Businessweek*, October 1, 1984, pp. 126–131.
26. "The New Calvinists: Are They Climbing the Ladder to Nowhere?" *The Indianapolis Star*, Tuesday, November 25, 1986, p. 16.
27. Ibid.

Notes to Pages 114–133

28. Ibid.
29. Ibid.
30. "The Party May Be Ending," *Fortune*, November 24, 1986, pp. 29–40.
31. Douglas Lamb and Glenn Reeder, "Reliving Golden Days," *Psychology Today*, June, 1986, pp. 22–30.
32. Ibid., p. 24.
33. Ibid., p. 26.
34. Ibid., p. 24.
35. Joan Liebman-Smith, "Sex: The Tyranny of Frequency, or When Enough is Enough," *Ms. Magazine*, April, 1987, pp. 78–89.
36. William Hartman and Marilyn Fithian, *Any Man Can*, (New York: St. Martin's Press, 1984).
37. Ibid., Fasteau.
38. Ibid., Fasteau, p. 27.

Chapter 4. Losers-Weepers: Dilemmas of the Underclass

1. Ruth Sidel, *Women and Children Last: The Plight of Poor Women in Affluent America* (New York: Viking Penguin, 1987).
2. Elliot Currie and Jerome Skolnick, *America's Problems: Social Issues and Public Policy* (Boston: Little, Brown and Co., 1984).
3. Ibid., p. 295.
4. Susan Shank and Steven Haugen, "The Employment Situation During 1986: Job Gains Continue, Unemployment Dips," *Monthly Labor Review*, February, Vol. 110, 1987, pp. 3–10.
5. Ibid., Currie and Skolnick, p. 309.
6. Joe R. Feagin, *Social Problems: A Critical Power Conflict Perspective* (Englewood Cliffs: Prentice-Hall, 1986).
7. Harry Braverman, *Labor and Monopoly Capital* (New York: Monthly Review Press, 1975).
8. Ivar Berg, *Education and Jobs: The Great Training Robbery* (New York: Praeger Publishers, 1970).
9. Barbara Ehrenreich, *Hearts of Men* (New York: Doubleday, 1983).

10. Ibid., Currie and Skolnick, p. 253.
11. Ibid., Sidel.
12. Ibid., p. 28.
13. Ibid., p. XVI.
14. Ibid., Feagin, p. 167.
15. Ibid.
16. Lillian Rubin, *Worlds of Pain* (New York: Basic Books, 1976).
17. Nicholas Lemann, "The Origins of the Underclass," *The Atlantic Monthly*, June, 1986, pp. 31–68.
18. Ibid., Sidel, p. 3.
19. Ibid., p. 24.
20. Ibid., p. 24.
21. Clifton R. Wharton, "'Demanding Families' and Black Achievement," *Education Week*, October 29, 1984, p. 24.
22. *Higher Education and National Affairs*, October 14, Vol. 34, No. 19, 1985, pp. 1–5.
23. Stan Warren, "A Generation of Talent America Can't Afford to Lose," *Cleveland Plain Dealer*, October 22, 1987, p. 11-c.
24. Reynolds Farley, *Blacks and Whites: Narrowing the Gap?* (Cambridge: Harvard University Press, 1984).
25. Randall Collins, *The Credential Society* (New York: Academic Press, 1979).
26. Kathy Hogan Trocheck, "Preschool Panic," *The Atlanta Constitution*, April 9, 1987, pp. 1–4B.
27. William Ryan, *Blaming the Victim* (New York: Random House, 1972).

Chapter 5. Toward a New Vision: The Emergence of the Productive Self

1. Erich Fromm, *The Sane Society* (New York: Reinhart, 1955).
2. Erich Fromm, *Escape From Freedom* (New York: Avon, 1965).
3. Ibid., Fromm, *The Sane Society*.
4. Ibid.
5. Christopher Lasch, *Haven in a Heartless World* (New York: Basic Books, 1977).

6. Ibid., p. 172.
7. Sheila Kitzinger, *Women as Mothers* (New York: Vintage Books, 1978).
8. Victor Goertzel and Mildred Goertzel, *Cradles of Eminence* (Boston: Little, Brown, 1962).
9. Samuel Bowles and Herbert Gintis, *Schooling in Capitalist America* (New York: Basic Books, 1976).
10. Ivan Illich, *Deschooling Society* (New York: Harper & Row, 1970).
11. Ibid., p. 39.
12. Ibid., p. 40.
13. Thomas Lasley and John Bregenzer, "Toward Selflessness," *Journal of Human Behavior and Learning*, Vol. 3, No. 2, 1986, pp. 20–27.
14. William Pink, "Creating Effective Schools," *Educational Forum*, Vol. 49, No. 1, 1984, pp. 91–107.
15. Ruth Steele, "Jefferson County Open High School — Philosophy and Purpose," *Holistic Education*, Vol. 1, No. 2, 1988, pp. 35–38.
16. Edward Clark, "The Search for a New Educational Paradigm," *Holistic Education*, Vol. 1, No. 1, 1988, pp. 18–30.
17. For two recent biographies of these men, see: Ronald Clark, *Einstein: The Life and Times* (New York: Avon, 1970); Robert Lacey, *Ford: The Men and the Machine* (New York: Ballantine, 1986).
18. Ibid., Edward Clark, p. 22.
19. Ivan Illich, *Tools for Conviviality* (New York: Harper & Row, 1973).
20. Robert Reich, *The Next American Frontier* (New York: Times Books, 1983).
21. Ibid., p. 20.
22. Ibid., p. 140.
23. David Bills, "Educational Credentials and Promotions: Does Schooling Do More Than Get You in the Door?" *Sociology of Education*, Vol. 61, January, 1988, pp. 52–60.
24. Martin Carnoy, Derek Shearer and Russell Rumsberger, *A New Social Contract* (New York: Harper & Row, 1983).